Situational Dialogues

MICHAEL OCKENDEN

The English Centre, Eastbourne

Illustrations by Malcolm Booker

LONGMAN

Contents

This situationally-graded book is intended for intermediate and advanced students wishing to learn and practise the type of informal conversational English in current, everyday use. Forty-four situations are presented, each in the form of four short dialogues. The aim of the student should be to memorise as many as possible of the expressions and phrases contained in the dialogues, since they are used by English people time and time again in the given situations.

DIALOGUES

Each situation is expressed by four dialogues arranged in parallel, so that any of A's first utterances may be followed by any of B's first utterances, and so on. This means that, with a 4 × 4 arrangement, we have 256 different variations of the same situation, leaving the class with a high degree of choice. Practice can be continued without boredom, and, by reading and acting out the dialogues many times in class and at home, the students painlessly learn the contents by heart.

DRILLS

These are based not on a grammatically graded sequence but on the dialogue situations and are intended to provide additional practice in some of the more important constructions. They should not be attempted one after the other, but done as a break between dialogue practice sessions.
In both drills and dialogues, stress marks ' are used to indicate emphasis.

KEY

A key to some of the harder drills is given at the end of the book; drills for which there is a key are marked thus:—*

INTONATION

The speaker's mental attitude is shown by the way in which the musical pitch of the voice changes. Three basic intonation tunes are used in English speech, each in various situations. These tunes may be broadly classified as:
(a) the falling tune
(b) the rising tune
(c) the falling-rising tune

(a) The falling tune
The voice falls from a high to a low note on one stressed syllable. It is used in the following cases:
1   in short complete statements
    It's 'not 'far.
2   for questions beginning with a question word
    'How much is this 'tie?
3   for question tags when the speaker is sure that what he says is right
    It's 'hot today, 'isn't it?
4   for orders and exclamations
    'Don't for'get.

(b) The rising tune
The voice rises on the last stressed word or on the unstressed syllables following the last stress. It is used in the following cases:
1   for statements intended to encourage
    'That's a good i'dea.
2   for questions which are answered by 'Yes' and 'No'
    Do you 'want to 'go?
    'Did you 'see the 'elephant?
3   for questions beginning with question words when the speaker wishes to show special interest
    'Where do you 'live?

4 for question tags when the speaker is not sure that what he says is correct
You 'know, 'don't you?
5 for sentences ending with 'please'; for 'goodbye'; for 'thank you' when it is used to show gratitude for a simple matter (passing the salt etc.)
What's the 'time, 'please?

(c) The falling-rising tune
The voice falls on the most important part of the sentence and rises again. It is used in the following cases:
1 for apologies
I'm 'sorry.
2 for expressing tentative opinions
I 'hope 'so.
The intonation of the sentences used in the dialogues follows the general rules above. The accompanying tapes should be listened to carefully and the intonation of the native speakers imitated.

CLASSROOM TECHNIQUE (4 × 4 dialogue)
1 The teacher reads aloud dialogue (i) and explains the meaning where necessary.
2 Class repeats dialogue (i) in chorus after the teacher. Some members are asked to read parts, again after the teacher.
3 The same procedure is followed for dialogue (ii).
4 The teacher points out to the class that there are sixteen (4 × 4) possible variations for the two dialogues covered so far.
5 The teacher takes the part of A and tells the best student to take that of B. Continue with other students, the teacher alternating between A and B. Students read both parts when everybody understands what is expected.
6 Continue as in 1, 2, and 5 for dialogues (iii) and (iv), explaining that there are now even more variations.

The large number of possibilities helps greatly to maintain class interest, but the teacher should vary the lesson as much as possible in order to prolong the practice to a point just below the threshold of boredom and restlessness (this will differ according to the motivation of the class, and the skill of the teacher, but somewhere between 20 and 30 minutes should be the target). There are several ways of doing this, such as:

(a) Constantly changing roles, teacher-student, student-teacher, student-student etc.
(b) Insisting that the students gradually increase the speed of delivery so that the dialogues always remain a challenge. A high degree of concentration is required of everybody, for nothing disrupts a smooth, rapid flow of exchanges so much as the student who loses the place and reads the wrong part.
(c) Reading rapidly non-stop round the class, each student saying one utterance only per dialogue, i.e.:
1st student: one of A's first utterances
2nd student: one of B's first utterances
3rd student: one of A's second utterances
4th student: one of B's second utterances
5th student: one of A's first utterances
etc.
The above procedure is continued for two or three circuits of the class. The teacher must insist on fast and accurate exchanges.
(d) Carrying out a conventional pattern practice of important structures using call-words, i.e.:
'Is there any chance of borrowing your umbrella?
tape-recorder / bicycle / hair-drier / etc.'
(e) Limiting the practice to the first two utterances of all four dialogues and insisting on rapid exchanges round the class.

(f) Asking the class to write out a dialogue from memory and then calling on certain members to read aloud their efforts.

(g) Asking students to act out a situation from memory.

(h) Playing the 'hangman' game with phrases from the current and previous dialogues: this is best done as a form of relaxation at the end of a hard practice session.

REVISION

It is important to spend a few minutes at the beginning of each lesson revising previous dialogues but since they are so short, the time required is minimal.

TAPES

These have been recorded with pauses making it possible for the student working alone *to hold a conversation* with his recorder.

Each of the forty-four situations has been recorded thus:

(a) Listening

All four dialogues straight through without pauses.

(b) Dialogue practice

For some situations the student is expected to take the part of A and for others that of B: whichever is more useful. The tape, acting the part of the other speaker, delivers a random selection of utterances and the student responds using one of the four alternatives available.

(c) Drills

Drills marked ◉ have been recorded; pauses are left for the students to take the parts of A or B as instructed on the tape.

Section (a) 'Listening' should be done with books shut.

Section (b) 'Dialogue Practice' should be done with books shut when the student is confident.

Section (c) 'Drills' have been recorded in such a way that they may be done with books shut.

CASSETTE

The dialogues are now available in cassette form.

I Asking the Way

Although all houses should have a street number, many are known only by a name. If you have difficulty in finding such a house, try asking the local shopkeepers or, better still, the postman, if you are lucky enough to see him. If you know that someone lives in a certain road but you do not know which number, ask at the public library or police station and they will check on the electoral roll. This is a road-by-road list of all the people entitled to vote.

	(i)	(ii)	(iii)	(iv)
A	Excuse me. Can you tell me where South Street is, please?	Excuse me, please. Could you tell me the way to the station?	Excuse me, but I'm trying to find the Town Hall.	Excuse me, please. Could you tell me how to get to the town centre?
B	Take the second on the left and then ask again.	Turn round and turn left at the traffic-lights.	Take the third on the right and go straight on.	First right, second left. You can't miss it.
A	Is it far?	Will it take me long to get there?	Should I take a bus?	Is it too far to walk?
B	No, it's only about five minutes' walk.	No, it's no distance at all.	No, you can walk it in under five minutes.	No, it's only a couple of hundred yards.
A	Many thanks.	Thank you.	Thank you very much indeed.	Thanks very much.
B	Not at all.	That's OK.	That's quite all right.	It's a pleasure.

I

Make sentences as in the example.

Example You take the second turning on the right after the traffic-lights.

1) .... zebra-crossing.
2) .... left ....
3) .... third ....
4) .... road ....
5) Go down.............. ....

2

Make questions and answers substituting for the items in bold type.

Example

STUDENT A Do I take the **second** on the **left**?

STUDENT B No, you want the **first** on the **right**.

I   A ...... second ...... right?
    B ...... first ...... left.
2   A ...... third ...... left?
    B ...... fourth ...... left.
3   A ...... third ...... right?
    B ...... second ...... left.
4   A ...... fourth ...... left?
    B ...... first ...... right.
5   A ...... next ...... right?
    B ...... next ...... left.

3 *◉

Change A's questions to a more polite form.

Example

STUDENT A Where's the station?

STUDENT B Can you tell me **where the station is**, please?

I   A How far is it to London?
    B ....?
2   A Where are the shops?
    B ....?
3   A Which direction is the motorway?[1]
    B ....?
4   A How many miles is it to the nearest garage?
    B ....?
5   A Which way's the coast?
    B ....?

4 *

Change A's statements as in the example.

Example

STUDENT A **He'll** get there in ten hours.

STUDENT B It'll take **him** ten hours to get there.

I   A She'll learn it in ten lessons.
    B ....

2   A They'll walk it in half an hour.
    B ....
3   A I'll make it in twenty minutes.
    B ....
4   A We'll deliver it in twenty-four hours.
    B ....
5   A You'll get there in less than a minute.
    B ....

5 *◉

Change A's statements as in the example.

Example

STUDENT A It's far: you can't walk.

STUDENT B It's too far to walk.

I   A It's foggy: you can't see the turning.
    B ....
2   A It's wet: you can't go on foot.
    B ....
3   A It's dark: you can't find the way.
    B ....
4   A It's late: you can't get there in time.
    B ....
5   A It's difficult: you can't remember.
    B ....

[1] motorway: a fast road, divided down the centre to separate cars going in different directions

3

2 On a Bus

Bus conductors still collect passengers' fares in most towns, but single-deck one-man buses are seen more and more, especially in country districts. In London, fast buses called 'Red Arrows' run non-stop between important places. The fare is fixed, and passengers pass through an automatic gate which opens when the correct coins are inserted.

	(i)	(ii)	(iii)	(iv)
A	Does this bus go to the station?	Am I OK for St Mary's Church?	Do you go to the sea-front?	Is this the right bus for the Town Hall?
B	No, you'll have to get off at the bank, and take a 192.[1]	No, we only go as far as the park, but you can walk from there.	No, you're going the wrong way. You want a 143 from the church.	No, you should have caught a 12. Jump out at the bridge and get one there.
A	Can you tell me where to get off?	How much further is it?	Have we got much further to go?	Could you tell me when we get there?
B	It's the next stop but one.[2]	'It's quite a way yet, but I'll tell you in good time.	It's the next stop.	It's three stops after this one.

[1] bus numbers such as 15 and 93 are pronounced as 'fifteen' and 'ninety-three'. Larger numbers such as 143 are pronounced as 'one-four-three'

[2] the next stop but one: two stops from here

I

Example

Would you tell me where I get off for St. Mary's Church, please?

1) .... Terminus Road, ...? ·
2) .... out ....? *
3) Could ....? *
4) .... the right stop ....? ·
5) .... Princes Park .....? .

2

Example

STUDENT A Does the **19** go to **Terminus Road**?

STUDENT B **Terminus Road**? No, it only goes as far as **the church!** You want a **91**!

1 A ...... 21 ...... the post office?
   B ...... the river ...... 12.
2 A ...... 152 ......the clock tower?
   B ...... Duke Street ...... 251.
3 A ...... 14 ...... Scampton?
   B ..... Waddington ...... 41.
4 A ...... 68 ...... the university?
   B ...... the Odeon ...... 86.
5 A ...... 72....the technical college?
   B ...... the castle ...... 27.

3*◉

Respond to A's statements using the phrase 'shouldn't have' plus the past participle.

Example

STUDENT A I **took the 61**!

STUDENT B You **shouldn't have taken the 61**! That was a mistake.

1 A I got out at the park.
   B ....
2 A I caught a Red Arrow.
   B ....
3 A I came early.
   B ....
4 A I asked for the station.
   B ....
5 A I bought a return ticket.
   B ....

4*

Respond to A's statements using the phrase 'should have' plus the past participle.

Example

STUDENT A I **didn't go by bus**!

STUDENT B That was wrong. You '**should have gone by bus**!

1 A I didn't remember the number.
   B ....
2 A I didn't bring my season ticket.
   B ....
3 A I didn't ring the bell.
   B ....
4 A I didn't have any change.
   B ....
5 A I didn't get a return.
   B ....

3 *Taking a Taxi*

London taxis carry meters indicating the fare to be paid. Drivers must charge the metered fare for all journeys within the London police districts, regardless of duration and distance, and including journeys to and from London Airport (Heathrow). Taxi drivers expect to be tipped for all journeys.

(i)	(ii)	(iii)	(iv)
A West London Air Terminal please. I have to be there by 11.10.	Do you think you can get me to Victoria by half past?	Piccadilly, please. I have an appointment at 10.30.	Paddington, please. I want to catch the 11.15.
B I can't promise, but I'll do my best.	We should be OK if the lights are with us.	I think we can make it[1] if we get a move on.[2]	We'll be all right if there are no hold-ups.[1]
B You're just in time. 70p,[1] please.	You've still got five minutes to spare. 70p, please.	Here we are, sir. 80p, please.	This is it, sir. 70p, please.
A Thanks a lot. Here's 80p. You can keep the change.	Thanks very much indeed. Here's a pound, give me 20p, please.	Many thanks. Let's call it a pound.	Thank you. Here's the fare, and this is for you.

[1] 70p: 70 new pence

[1] make it: get there in time
[2] get a move on: hurry

[1] hold-ups: delays

1

Example
> My conference is at eleven-thirty so I want to be there at eleven.

1) .... eleven-fifteen ....
2) ... meeting ....
3) .... set out ....
4) .... at eight.
5) .... be called ....

2

Example
STUDENT A Do you think you can get me to **Victoria by half past?**
STUDENT B We should make it **if the lights are green!**

1   A ...... the station by half past?
    B ...... if the lights are with us.
2   A ...... the Hilton Hotel by eleven?
    B ...... if the traffic's not too heavy.
3   A .... Waterloo by twenty-five past?
    B .... unless we get held up.
4   A .... the French Embassy by 2.15?
    B .... unless the lights are against us.
5   A .... this address by ten to?
    B .... unless we get caught in the rush hour.[1]

3

It is possible to give a tip by asking for a certain amount of change.

Example (A tip of 10 new pence)
STUDENT A **70p** please.
STUDENT B Right. Here's **a pound!** Give me **20p** change, please.

1   A 20p ......
    B ...... 50p ...... 25p ......

2   A 40p ......
    B ...... 50p ...... 5p ......
3   A £1.25[2] ......
    B ...... £1.50 ...... 10p ......
4   A 64p ......
    B ...... a pound ...... 30p ......
5   A 14p ......
    B ...... 20p ...... 4p ......

4

Reply to A's questions using 'I want to' followed by the correct verb.

Example
STUDENT A Which train are you **catching?**
STUDENT B I want to **catch the 11.45!**

1   A What time are you setting out?
    B ...... at two o'clock.
2   A How long are you staying?
    B ...... for an hour.
3   A Which station are you going to?
    B ...... Waterloo.
4   A Which part of London are you going to?
    B ...... Hampstead.
5   A When are you coming back?
    B ...... at twelve.

5

Example
STUDENT A **You'll** never make it by **ten!**
STUDENT B There's no rush.[3] I don't have to be there till **10.30.**

1   A He ...... eleven.
    B .... 11.30.
2   A They ...... twelve.
    B .... 12.30.
3   A We ...... one.
    B .... 1.30.
4   A She ...... four.
    B .... 4.30.
5   A I ...... six.
    B .... 6.30.

[1] the rush hour: the time when people are going to and from work
[2] £1.25: pronounced 'one pound twenty-five' or one twenty-five
[3] there's no rush: there is no need to hurry

4 *At a Railway Station*

The normal return ticket costs double the single fare but cheaper return tickets called 'Day Returns' may be bought at most stations. These tickets are ideal for one-day excursions to London, although certain trains may not be used. There is no extra charge in the U.K. for travel on express trains except on some trains called 'Pullmans'.

	(i)	(ii)	(iii)	(iv)
A	When does the London train leave, please?	Which train do I take for Victoria, please?	Which platform for London Bridge, please?	What time's the next train to Victoria, please?
B	9.25. Platform 3.	9.28. This end of Platform 2.	9.27 from Platform 1.	9.26. Platform 4. Right up at the front.
A	What time does it reach London?	When does it get in?	What time does it arrive?	When do we get there?
B	You should be there at 11.31, but you may be a bit late.	It gets there at 11.34.	It takes roughly two hours so you'll arrive just before 11.30.	It's due in at 11.35, but they're running late today.
A	Do I have to change?	Must I change?	Is it necessary to change?	Need I change trains?
B	Yes. You change at Lewes and East Croydon.	No. It's a through train.[1]	No. There's no need to change.	Yes. Change at East Croydon.

[1] a through train: a train which takes you to your destination without a change

1

Example

Three first class singles to London, please.

1) .... Bexhill ......
2) A three-month return ....
3) Two Day Returns ....
4) .... Brighton ......
5) A single ....

2

Example

Which **side of the platform** do I want for **Newhaven Harbour**, please?

1 ...... part of the train .... Charing Cross, ...?
2 .... platform .... Dover Marine ....?
3 .... carriage .... Eastbourne ....?
4 .... station .... Hastings ....?
5 ...... train .... Tilbury........?

3

Example

STUDENT A Which train would get me to **York** by **4.30**?

STUDENT B If you caught the **11.35**, you'd be there at **16.14**.

1 A ...... Victoria .. 8.30 a.m.?
  B ...... 7.12 ...... 8.11.
2 A ...... Paris .. six thirty?
  B ...... 9.50 ...... 18.07.
3 A ...... Hastings .. 5.45?
  B ...... 5.10 ...... 5.40.
4 A ...... Leeds .. 7.00 p.m.?
  B ...... 13.36 ...... 18.40.
5 A ... Tilbury .. midday?
  B ... 7.27 ...... 11.34.

4

Example

STUDENT A Need **I** change at **Crewe**?

STUDENT B No, **you don't** have to change till **Grantham**.

1 A ..... he ...... Lewes?
  B ...... East Croydon.
2 A ..... they ...... Swindon?
  B .... Bristol.
3 A ..... she ...... Winchester?
  B .... Southampton.
4 A ..... we ...... Cambridge?
  B .... Ely.
5 A ..... I ...... Haywards Heath?
  B ..... Three Bridges.

5

Example

STUDENT A When does the **9.15** get to **Victoria**?

STUDENT B The **9.15**? It's due in at **10.32**.

1 A .... 8.33 .... Waterloo?
  B .... 9.10.
2 A .... 7.27 .... Tunbridge Wells?
  B .... 9.48.
3 A .... 3.45 .... Leeds?
  B .... 18.58.
4 A .... 12.35 .... Lincoln?
  B .... 21.20.
5 A .. midnight train .. Eastbourne?
  B .... 1.11.

5 The London Underground

Fares on the London Underground (the Tube) are not fixed, but are proportional to the distance travelled. There are nine lines in the system: the Bakerloo, Central, Circle, District, Metropolitan, Northern, Piccadilly, Victoria and Waterloo and City lines.

	(i)	(ii)	(iii)	(iv)
A	Which way do I go for Queensway, please?	How do I get to Lancaster Gate, please?	Which line do I take for Marble Arch, please?	Can you tell me the best way to get to Bond Street, please?
B	Take the Bakerloo to Paddington; the District to Notting Hill and then get the Central.	Catch the Metropolitan to Liverpool Street and then change to the Central Line.	That's easy; it's the next station down the Central Line.	You want the Victoria to Oxford Circus and then you change on to the Central.
A	Where do I go now?	Which platform do I want?	How do I get down to the trains?	Which way do I go first?
B	Take the escalator on your right.	Follow those signs. You can't go wrong.	Get that lift over there.	Go straight down the stairs, and turn left at the bottom.

I

Example

Go straight down the escalator and follow the signs to Waterloo.

1) .... up   ....
2) .... Victoria..
3) .... up in the lift   ....
4) .... arrows ....
5) .... Kings Cross.

2⊚

Example

STUDENT A Can you tell me the best way to get to **Holborn**, please?

STUDENT B Take the **Bakerloo** to **Oxford Circus** and change to the **Central**.

1 A ...... Earls Court ......?
   B .... Metropolitan .... Hammersmith .... District.
2 A ...... Knightsbridge ......?
   B .... Circle .... South Kensington .... Piccadilly.
3 A ...... Regents Park ......?
   B .... Victoria .... Oxford Circus .... Bakerloo.
4 A ...... Baker Street ......?
   B .... Northern .... Aldersgate .. .... Metropolitan.
5 A ...... Liverpool Street ......?
   B .... Waterloo and City .... the Bank .... Central.

3

Example

STUDENT A Excuse me, but is this the right **train** for St Pauls?

STUDENT B Yes, it's **three stops** down the line.

1 A ... platform ... Leicester Square?
   B ...... two stops ......
2 A .... side .... Marble Arch?
   B .... the next stop ......
3 A .... line .... Holland Park?
   B ...... four stops ......
4 A .... direction .... Swiss Cottage?
   B ...... the stop after next ......

4⊚

Example

STUDENT A Excuse me, please. Which way do I go for **Notting Hill**?

STUDENT B **Notting Hill**? Take the **lift** down to the **Central** Line.

1 A ...... Piccadilly Circus?
   B .... escalator .... Bakerloo ....
2 A ...... Tower Hill?
   B .... stairs .... Circle ....
3 A ...... Bayswater?
   B .... lift .... District ....
4 A ...... Waterloo?
   B .... stairs .... Northern ....
5 A ...... Arsenal?
   B .... escalator .... Piccadilly ....

6 Booking Airline Tickets

There are two London Airports: Heathrow and Gatwick. The former is the main one, but the latter is nearer to the south coast.

(i)

A I want to fly to Geneva on or about the first.

B I'll just see what there is.

A I want to go economy, and I'd prefer the morning.

B Lufthansa Flight LH 203 leaves at 0920.

A What time do I have to be there?

B The coach leaves for the airport at 0815.

(ii)

A I'd like to book a flight to Munich for Monday the tenth.

B I'll have a look in the time-table for you.

A I'll need an economy class open return.[1]

B KLM have got a DC-9 leaving at 0925.

A What else ought I to know?

B The latest time of reporting is 0835 at the airport.

(iii)

A What flights are there from London to Vienna to-morrow?

B If you'd like to take a seat, I'll find out for you.

A I'd like to travel first class, please.

B BEA Flight BE 502 takes off from Heathrow at 0925, and flies direct.

A What time have I got to get there?

B You'll have to be at West London Air Terminal by 0810 at the latest.

(iv)

A Are there any planes to Zürich on a Sunday?

B If you'll excuse me for a second, I'll check.

A By the way, I don't want a night flight.

B There's a Swissair Trident out of London at 0920.

A When am I supposed to check in?

B If you're going to the airport, you must be there before 0835.

[1] open return: a return which may be used at any time

1

Example

    Is it possible to break my journey at Athens on my way to Istanbul?

1) .... stay a night   ....?
2) ....Rome ....?
3) .... stop over   ....?
4) Is it all right...........   ....?
5) .... Teheran?

2⊚

Example

STUDENT A Can I break my journey to **Delhi**?

STUDENT B Yes, you can stop over at **Teheran** if you like.

1 A .... Chicago?
   B ...... New York ......
2 A .... Kuwait?
   B ...... Beirut ......
3 A .... Miami?
   B ...... Shannon ......
4 A .... Cairo?
   B I-...... Orly ......
5 A .... Karachi?
   B ...... Rome ......

3

Example

STUDENT A Which flight gets me to **Beirut** by **7 p.m.**?

STUDENT B **BEA Flight 254** departs at **1030** and arrives at **1235**.

1 A ...... Geneva ...... midnight?
   B Swissair Flight SR 871 .... 2220 .... 2340.
2 A ...... Rotterdam ...... 7 p.m.?
   B KLM Flight KL 106 ...... 1705 ...... 1800.
3 A ...... Stuttgart ...... 5 p.m.?
   B Lufthansa Flight LH 243 ...... 1500 ...... 1625.
4 A ...... Oslo ...... 10 p.m.?
   B SAS Flight SK 512 ...... 1935 ...... 2130.
5 A ...... Madrid ...... lunchtime?
   B BEA Flight BE 048 ...... 1030 ...... 1255.

4

Example

STUDENT A What **night** flights are there from **Gatwick** to **Copenhagen** to-morrow?

STUDENT B **SAS** have got a **Caravelle** leaving at **4.30**.

1 A .... morning .... Heathrow .... Zürich ....?
   B Swissair .... DC-9 .... 0850.
2 A .... afternoon .... Manchester .... Amsterdam ....?
   B KLM .... 1-11 .... 1700.
3 A .... night economy .... London .... Paris ....?
   B BEA .... Trident .... 2200.
4 A .... tourist .... London .... Frankfurt ....?
   B Lufthansa .... 707 .... 1710.
5 A .... evening .... Malta .... Birmingham ....?
   B BEA .... Trident .... 2115.

7 Hiring a Car

Foreign visitors may use their foreign licences for a period of one year before they have to take the British driving test. An international licence is not normally necessary.

	(i)	(ii)	(iii)	(iv)
A	How much is it to hire an Imp?	What's the rate for one of your Minis?	Can you tell me the hire charge for 1100's,[1] please?	Suppose I wanted to hire a Mini van – how much would it cost?
B	£2.75 a day or £15.50 a week.	The daily rate is £2.20, and the weekly £15.	You can have one for £2.90 a day, or £16.50 for a week.	£2.80 per day, £16 per week.
A	Will I be able to have one next weekend?	Right then. I'd like to book one for next Friday, please.	All right. I'll take one for the week starting Tuesday next.	Fair enough.[1] Reserve me one from the 1st to the 10th, please.
B	Have you got a current[1] licence?	Is yours a full licence?	Is your driving licence valid?[2]	Have you held a licence for over two years?
A	Yes, I've been driving since I was eighteen.	Yes, I've had one ever since 1968.	Yes, it doesn't expire till next year.	Yes, I renewed it yesterday.
B	Good. All you do now is complete this form.	OK. If you'll just fill up this form, I'll book you one.	Fine. We'll need some particulars and a five-pound deposit.	Right. In that case there's only a form to fill in.

[1] a current licence: an up-to-date licence

[1] an 1100: an eleven hundred (a popular British car)
[2] a valid licence: an up-to-date licence

[1] fair enough: that's all right

Drills

1

Example

Can you hire me a Mini for three days from tomorrow?

1) .... an Imp ....?
2) .... rent ....?
3) .... six ....?
4) .... next Monday?
5) .... an 1100 ....?

2

Example

STUDENT A Is there a **Mini** for hire next **Monday?**

STUDENT B The best I can do is an **1100**. All the **Minis** are out till **Wednesday.**

1 A ...... Escort ...... Saturday?
   B ...... Cortina ..... Escorts ..... Monday.
2 A ...... Viva ...... Tuesday?
   B .... Maxi .... Vivas .... Friday.
3 A .... Imp ...... Thursday?
   B ... Cresta ... Imps ... Sunday.
4 A ...... Herald ...... Wednesday?
   B ... VW ... Heralds ... Saturday.
5 A ...... Victor ...... Sunday?
   B .. Avenger .. Victors .. Monday.

3

Example

STUDENT A What's the **daily** rate for a **Mini?**

STUDENT B They're **£2.75** a day.

1 A ...... weekly ...... 1100?
   B £15.00 ....
2 A ...... hourly ...... chauffeured Rolls?
   B £3.50 ....
3 A ...... monthly ...... Escort?
   B £56.00 ....
4 A ...... fortnightly ...... Viva?
   B £29.00 ....
5 A ...... weekend ...... Cortina?
   B £6.00 ....

15

8 At a Garage

There is no need to tip the petrol pump attendant unless he has been especially helpful. Some garages offer green or pink trading stamps with petrol in order to encourage people to buy; these stamps can be exchanged for goods at special shops when enough have been collected. Never refuse stamps if they are offered because your English friends will be very grateful for them.

(i)

A Three and a half gallons of super and a pint of oil, please.

B Right, sir. Shall I check the tyres?

A No, thanks. I'm in a bit of a hurry. How much do I owe you?

B That'll be £1.34, sir.

(ii)

A A pound's worth of super, and top up the oil,[1] please.

B Certainly, sir. How about your radiator?

A Thanks, but I can't stop now. How much is that?

B £1.30, please.

(iii)

A Four gallons of regular[1] and some oil, please.

B All right, sir. Do you want your windscreen cleaned, too?

A No, thanks. I'm a little late. What does it come to?

B £1.32 in all, please.

(iv)

A Fill her[1] up, please.

B With pleasure, sir. Would you like me to look at the battery?

A Not now, thanks. How much, please?

B £1.33, please.

[1] top up the oil: pour in more oil to bring it to the correct level

[1] regular: minimum grade for most British cars

[1] her: many people refer to their cars as 'her'

I

Example
> Would you look at the battery and clean the windscreen, please?

1) Could ....?
2) .... the tyres ....?
3) .... the headlights .....?
4) .... check ....?
5) .... the oil .. ..?

2◉

Example
STUDENT A Shall I have a look at the **tyres**?
STUDENT B Yes, and could you check the **battery** as well, please?

1 A .... radiator?
  B ...... oil ......?
2 A .... battery?
  B ...... anti-freeze ......?
3 A .... brake fluid?
  B ..... windscreen washers .....?
4 A .... spare wheel?
  B .... stop lights .....?
5 A .... water?
  B ...... tyres ......?

3

Example
STUDENT A How much do I owe you for the **petrol**?
STUDENT B With the **oil**, **£1.32** in all, please.

1 A .... anti-freeze?
  B ...... new tyre, £8.55 ......
2 A .... service?
  B ..... parts, £4.80 ......
3 A .... headlight?
  B ..... labour, £2.75 ......
4 A .... car-wash?
  B ...... waxing, £1.10 ......
5 A .... roof-rack?
  B ...... fitting, £2.75 ......

4*◉

Answer A's questions using the phrase 'to be in a hurry'.

Example
STUDENT A Why **can't you** wait?
STUDENT B Because **I'm in a hurry.**

1 A ...... couldn't you ...... ?
  B ....
2 A ...... couldn't they ...... ?
  B ....
3 A ..... can't she ...... ?
  B ....
4 A ...... can't they ...... ?
  B ....
5 A ...... couldn't he ...... ?
  B ....
6 A ..... can't we ......?
  B ....
7 A ...... couldn't we ......?
  B ....

Drills

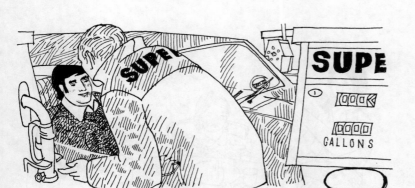

9 At Lunch

Although the correct name for the midday meal is lunch, many English families call it 'dinner'. To complicate matters further, the mid-morning break of coffee and biscuits is also called 'lunch'. English people do not wish each other 'Good Appetite'.

(i)	(ii)	(iii)	(iv)
A You 'must have some more chicken.	Wouldn't you like to finish up the omelette?	Another piece of meat pie?	'Do have the rest of the mashed potato.
B No, thanks. I'm supposed to be slimming.	No, 'really, thank you. I just couldn't eat any more.	No, thanks, really. I'm on a diet.	No, thank you. I've had too much already.
A Can't I tempt you?	Come on now. Surely you can manage it.	'Please do. You've hardly eaten anything.	Just take it to please me.
B Well, maybe I 'could manage a very small piece.	No, thank you, really. I must have put on pounds as it is.	It's delicious, but I don't think I ought to.	OK, but only a small piece or I shan't have room for any pudding.

I

Example
It's very tasty but I honestly couldn't manage another piece.
1) ... delicious ....:...
2) .... really ....
3) .... any more.
4) ... very nice ....
5) .... just ....

2◉

Example
STUDENT A Surely you can eat **another piece of cake**.
STUDENT B Well, maybe I 'could manage just **a very small piece**.

1 A ...... the rest of the lamb.
   B .... a little.
2 A ...... some more potatoes.
   B .... one or two.
3 A ..... another slice of toast.
   B .... one more.
4 A ...... some more trifle.¹
   B .... a little more.
5 A ...... that last fish finger.²
   B .... half of it.

3*◉

Answer A's questions using 'too much' or 'too many'.

Example
STUDENT A You 'must have some more **rice**.
STUDENT B No, thanks, really. I've had 'far **too much** already.

1 A .... potatoes.
   B ....

2 A .... wine.
   B ....
3 A .... carrots.
   B ....
4 A .... meat.
   B ....
5 A .... ice-cream.
   B ....

4

Example
STUDENT A Wouldn't you like some more **trifle?**
STUDENT B Yes, I'd love some. It's a **delicious trifle**.

1 A .... pudding?
   B ...... lovely ......
2 A .... pie?
   B ...... gorgeous ......
3 A .... salad?
   B ...... delicious ......
4 A .... stew?
   B ...... very nice ......
5 A .... wine?
   B ...... excellent ......

5*

Example
STUDENT A Did he **say** much?
STUDENT B No, he hardly **said** anything.

1 A ...... they want ......?
   B ....
2 A ...... he drink ......?
   B ....
3 A ...... she eat ......?
   B ....
4 A ...... it cost ......?
   B ....
5 A ...... I get ......?
   B ....

¹ trifle: a pudding made with cake, fruit, cream and sherry
² fish fingers: frozen pieces of fish sold in packets.

10 Tea-time

The English drink more tea than any other nation – 7.77 pounds per year or 4.67 cups daily per head. In times of disaster or tragedy 'a nice cup of tea' is offered as a kind of universal cure.

	(i)	(ii)	(iii)	(iv)
A	Would you care for a cup of tea?	I expect you could do with a cup of tea, couldn't you?	How about a nice cup of tea before you go?	Would you like a cup of tea?
B	Only if 'you're having one.	I'd rather have a cup of coffee, if you don't mind.	Yes, I'd love one.	Only if it's not too much trouble.
A	Do you take milk and sugar?	Milk and sugar?	How do you like it?	Do you like it with milk and sugar?
B	A dash of milk[1] and two lumps,[2] please.	A milky one without sugar, please.	A strong one with three spoons for me, please.	Not too much milk and just half a spoonful, please.

[1] a dash of milk: a very little milk
[2] two lumps: two sugar cubes

Drills

1

Example

Plenty of milk and three spoons for me, please.

1) .... lumps ....
2) A dash of.............. ....
3) .... no sugar ....
4) A little.............. ....
5) .... lots of sugar ....

2◉

Example

STUDENT A Would you care for **a cup of tea?**

STUDENT B I'd rather have **a cup of coffee,** if you don't mind.

1 A ...... a chocolate biscuit?
  B ...... a cream cake ......
2 A ...... a glass of milk?
  B ...... a drink of orange ......
3 A ...... a cucumber sandwich?
  B ...... a muffin[1] ......
4 A ...... a slice of cake?
  B ...... a doughnut[2] ......
5 A ...... another piece of toast?
  B ...... a sausage roll ......

3

Reply to A's questions using the second alternative.

Example

STUDENT A Do you like **tea** or would you prefer **coffee?**

STUDENT B **Coffee** for me, please.

1 A ...... jam ...... fishpaste?
  B ....
2 A ...... cake ...... biscuits?
  B ....
3 A ...... toast ...... bread?
  B ....
4 A ...... milk ...... lemon?
  B ....
5 A ...... white bread ...... brown?
  B ....

4*◉

Reply to A's questions using 'one', 'some', 'it', 'them', or 'to'.

Example

STUDENT A Would you like **a cup of tea?**
STUDENT B I'd love **one.**

1 A ...... this sandwich?
  B ....
2 A ...... some coffee?
  B ....
3 A ...... these biscuits?
  B ....
4 A ...... to come again?
  B ....
5 A ...... another bun?[3]
  B ....

5◉

An informal way of saying 'I need a cup of tea' is to say 'I could do with a cup of tea.' Make A's statements more informal.

Example

STUDENT A I need **a new set of tyres.**
STUDENT B I could do with **a new set of tyres.**

1 A I need a cup of tea.
  B ....
2 A Patrick needs a haircut.
  B ....
3 A They need a few days off.
  B ....
4 A Your front door needs a coat of paint.
  B ....
5 A Mother needs a holiday.
  B ....

[1] a muffin: a toasted cake eaten with butter
[2] a doughnut: a cake made of dough, sweetened and fried
[3] a bun: a cake made with yeast

21

11 *With a Friend in a Coffee Bar*

Coffee bars are popular meeting places for young people. It is possible to dance in some bars, but alcoholic drinks are not sold.

	(i)	(ii)	(iii)	(iv)
A	What would you like to drink?	What can I get you to drink?	What are you going to have to drink?	What do you want to drink?
B	A black coffee for me, please.	An iced Coke[1] would go down well.	I'd like something cool.	I feel like a cup of tea.
A	How about something to eat?	Wouldn't you like some cake, too?	Would you care for some cake?	Do you fancy something to eat?
B	Yes, I'd love a portion of that strawberry tart.	Yes, I think I'll have a slice of chocolate sponge.	Yes, I'll try a piece of cheese cake.	Yes, I'd rather like some of that fruit cake.
A	Right. I'll see if I can catch the waitress's eye.	Right. Sit down there and I'll bring it over.	It certainly looks tempting. I wouldn't mind some my-self.[1]	That's a good idea. I think I'll join you.

[1] Coke: Coca Cola   [1] I wouldn't mind: I'd rather like

I

Example

Would you care for a round of ham sandwiches and a cup of tea?

1) . . . . a milk shake?
2) Wouldn't you like . . . . ?
3) . . . . a piece of cheese cake . . . . ?
4) . . . . fruit . . . . ?
5) Do you fancy . . . . ?

2 ⊚

Example

STUDENT A I think I'll have **a coffee.**
STUDENT B That's a good idea. **Coffee** for
'me, too, please.

1 A . . . . . . a Coke.
   B . . . .
2 A . . . . . . a tea.
   B . . . .
3 A . . . . . . a chocolate.
   B . . . .
4 A . . . . . . a Horlicks.[1]
   B . . . .
5 A . . . . . . a milk.
   B . . . .

3

Example

STUDENT A This **jam sponge** is absolutely
delicious.
STUDENT B Yes, it looks it. I wouldn't
mind a **slice** myself.

1 A . . . . . raspberry milk shake . . . . .
   B . . . . . . a glass . . . . . .

2 A . . . . . . toasted sandwiches . . . . . .
   B . . . . . . a round . . . . . .
3 A . . . . . . chocolate cakes . . . . . .
   B . . . . . . a couple . . . . . .
4 A . . . . . . coffee ice-cream . . . . . .
   B . . . . . . one . . . . . .
5 A . . . . . . hot chocolate . . . . . .
   B . . . . . . a cup . . . . . .

4

Example

STUDENT A Would you care for **a piece of
cake?**
STUDENT B Yes, please. The **chocolate
sponge** looks rather tempting.

1 A . . . . . . something to drink?
   B . . . . . . iced Coke . . . . . .
2 A . . . . . . a toasted sandwich?
   B . . . . . cheese and bacon . . . . . .
3 A . . . . . . something to eat?
   B . . . . . . strawberry tarts . . . . . .
4 A . . . . . . an ice-cream?
   B . . . . . . chocolate . . . . . .
5 A . . . . . . a cake?
   B . . . . . . cream doughnuts . . . . . .

5 *

The word 'glass', 'cup' etc is often omitted
when you are ordering drinks.

Example

STUDENT A Tell the waitress we want **two
cups of tea and a glass of lemonade.**
STUDENT B **Two teas, and a lemonade**
please.

1 A . . . . . . two cups of tea and a cup of
coffee.
   B . . . .
2 A . . . . . . a glass of Coca Cola and
four cups of tea.
   B . . . .
3 A . . . . . three cups of chocolate and
two glasses of orange juice.
   B . . . .
4 A . . . . . . a glass of orange juice and
two glasses of milk.
   B . . . .
5 A . . . . . . three cups of black coffee.
   B . . . .

Drills

[1] Horlicks: a malted milk drink

12 *In a Restaurant*

Inexpensive restaurants known as 'Fish and Chip Shops' are something of a national institution in the U.K. Remaining open until about 11 p.m., they are ideal for the motorist on a long journey. Fish and chips can be eaten in the restaurant or taken away wrapped in paper.

Foreign visitors to the U.K. are often surprised to see the large number of Chinese restaurants – at least one in every town. These restaurants offer good food at reasonable prices and are very popular.

	(i)	(ii)	(iii)	(iv)
A	Can I take your order, sir?	Have you decided on something, sir?	Have you chosen something, sir?	May I take your order, sir?
B	Yes. I'd like to try the steak, please.	Yes. Haddock[1] and chips for me, please.	Yes, I think I'll have the curry, please.	I'll just take a small salad, please.
A	And to follow?	How about the sweet?	What would you like afterwards?	Do you want any sweet?
B	Ice-cream, please.	No sweet thanks. Just coffee.	I'd like some fruit if you have any.	Apple pie and custard would be nice.

[1] haddock: a kind of fish

I

Example

I'll have grapefruit juice to begin with, and hamburger and chips to follow.

1) .... egg-mayonnaise .... a mushroom omelette ....
2) .... prawn cocktail .... grilled lamb chops ....
3) .... tomato juice .... a ham salad ....
4) .... onion soup .... beef curry ....
5) .... melon .... Irish stew ....

2

Example

STUDENT A And what will you have to follow the **soup**?

STUDENT B I think I'll try the **curry**, please.

1   A ...... fruit juice?
     B ...... fish ......
2   A ...... crab?
     B ...... chicken ......
3   A ...... prawn cocktail?
     B ...... steak ......
4   A ...... melon?
     B ...... beef ......
5   A ...... scampi?
     B ...... lamb ......

3◉

Example

STUDENT A Has **he** decided on something yet?

STUDENT B No, **he** can't make up **his** mind.

1   A ...... they ......?
     B ....
2   A ...... Margaret ......?
     B ....
3   A ...... Brian ......?
     B ....
4   A ...... you ......?
     B ....
5   A ...... the children ......?
     B ....

4*◉

Reply to A's questions using the present perfect tense.

Example

STUDENT A Would you like to **order your wine**, sir?

STUDENT B I've already **ordered** it, thank you very much.

1   A ...... have your soup ....?
     B ....
2   A ...... see the menu ....?
     B ....
3   A ...... book your table ....?
     B ....
4   A ...... taste the wine ....?
     B ....
5   A ...... choose your sweet ....?
     B ....

13 In a Pub

The hours during which English pubs are allowed to open are strictly controlled by the law. Times vary in different parts of the country, but are approximately from 11 a.m. to 2.30 p.m. and from 6 p.m. to 10.30 or 11 p.m. on weekdays, and from 12 noon to 2 p.m. and from 7.00 to 10.30 p.m. on Sundays. Beer, wine and spirits, as well as non-alcoholic drinks like lemonade can be bought at a pub, but it is rare to find one that sells coffee and tea. At one time, the only food available was sandwiches and meat pies but nowadays the situation is much better with salads and hot meats served at the bars of many pubs. Look outside for the signs 'INN FOOD' and 'PUB FOOD'. It is normal to buy one's own drinks at the bar, and the barman is not tipped unless he brings drinks to the table. Each order is paid for separately, and not at the end of the evening.

(i)	(ii)	(iii)	(iv)
A What are you going to have?	What's it to be?	What would you like to drink?	What can I get you?
B A half of bitter,[1] please.	The same again, please.	Just a light ale for me, please.	I'd like a lager, please.
A Are you sure you won't have a scotch?	Won't you make it a pint this time?	Won't you have a gin and tonic with me?	Wouldn't you care for something a little stronger?
B Thanks very much, but I'm driving.	I'd better not, thank you all the same.	That's very kind of you, but I don't think I will.	No, I think I'd better stick to halves,[1] thanks.

[1] a bitter: a light draught beer

[1] stick to halves: continue to drink half pints of beer

I

Example

Here's to a safe journey home.   Cheers!¹

1) .... good luck at the interview ......!
2) .... fine weather on holiday   ......!
3) .... the best of luck on Friday ......!
4) .... success in the exams   ......!

2⊚

Reply to A's questions saying: 'No, this is 'my round.'² and repeating his question.

Example

STUDENT A What are you going to have?
STUDENT B No, this is 'my round. What are 'you going to have?

1   A What would you like to drink?
    B ....
2   A What are you drinking?
    B ....
3   A What will you have?
    B ....
4   A What are you going to drink?
    B ....
5   A What are you having?
    B ....

3

Example

STUDENT A I'd like **a lager,** please.
STUDENT B Why don't you make it **a scotch?**

1   A .... a half ......
    B .... a pint?

2   A ...... a Coke ......
    B .... something stronger?
3   A ...... a light ale ......
    B .... a gin and tonic?
4   A ...... a pint of bitter ......
    B .... a brandy?
5   A ...... a shandy³ ......
    B .... a sherry?

4*⊚

Reply to A's questions using the correct auxiliary verb.

Example

STUDENT A Didn't he order **a bitter?**
STUDENT B **A bitter?** No, I don't 'think **he did.**

1   A Don't they close at eleven?
    B ....
2   A Wasn't his a shandy?
    B ....
3   A Doesn't she like Babycham?⁴
    B ....
4   A Haven't they got draught lager?
    B ....
5   A Isn't there an extension?⁵
    B ....

5

Respond to A's statement using the phrase 'Then you'd better' plus a question tag.

Example

STUDENT A I've got a shocking hangover.
STUDENT B Then you'd better **take an Alka-Seltzer,**⁶ hadn't you?

1   A I've been asked to bring a bottle.
    B ..... call at the off-licence⁷ .....?
2   A I've got to go in five minutes.
    B ...... drink up ......?
3   A I'm driving home.
    B ...... make this your last ......?
4   A I've brought the children.
    B ..... sit out in the garden .....?
5   A I've just won £5.
    B ...... buy a round ......?

¹ cheers: this is said before drinking
² my round: my turn to buy drinks
³ a shandy: beer and lemonade or ginger beer
⁴ Babycham: an inexpensive champagne-type drink
⁵ an extension: an extension of drinking hours
⁶ Alka-Seltzer: a kind of medicine
⁷ an off-licence: a place where alcoholic drinks may be bought but not drunk

14 *Offering Cigarettes*

Cigarettes are rather expensive in the U.K. as they carry a heavy tax. It is therefore a good idea to buy some duty-free ones on the plane or ship before arriving. The Customs allow approximately 200 to be brought in by each person over the age of seventeen.

	(i)	(ii)	(iii)	(iv)
A	Cigarette?	Have a cigarette.	Would you like a cigarette?	Help yourself to a cigarette.
B	No, thanks. Not before lunch.	No, thanks. I've just put one out.	No, thanks. I'm trying to cut down.	No, thanks. I'm trying to give up.
A	Please have one. It's a new brand.	Please do. I always seem to be smoking yours.	Go on. I owe you one from yesterday.	Come on. I insist.
B	I honestly don't feel like one at the moment, thanks.	Perhaps I will then. Have you got a light?[1]	OK, but next time you must have one of mine.	No, really, thank you. I've got a bit of a cough.

[1] a light: a match or a lighter

I

Example

Sorry to trouble you, but can you oblige me with a match?

1) .... give me ....?
2) .... have you got ....?
3) Excuse me, ...?
4) .... a light?
5) .... but could I trouble you for ......?

2

Example

STUDENT A Have a cigarette.
STUDENT B No, thanks. I never smoke **before lunch**.

1 A Cigarette?
   B ...... after meals.
2 A Help yourself to a cigarette.
   B ...... before breakfast.
3 A Would you like a cigarette?
   B ...... while I'm driving.
4 A Won't you have a cigarette?
   B ...... them without filters.
5 A Would you care for a cigarette?
   B ...... at work.

3*◉

Reply to A's questions reversing the pronouns.

Example

STUDENT A Did **he** smoke one of **yours**?
STUDENT B No, **I** smoked one of **his**.

1 A Did she smoke one of mine?
   B ....
2 A Did they smoke one of his?
   B ....
3 A Did we smoke one of theirs?
   B ....
4 A Did I smoke one of hers?
   B ....
5 A Did she smoke one of his?
   B ....

4*

You can say: 'I've stopped smoking' or 'I've given up smoking'. You can say: 'I've smoked less' or 'I've cut down my smoking'.
Reply to A's questions using the correct form of 'give up' or 'cut down'.

Example (1)

STUDENT A Are you smoking less?
STUDENT B Yes, I'm cutting down.

Example (2)

STUDENT A Have you stopped smoking?
STUDENT B Yes, I've given up.

1 A Have you smoked less?
   B ....
2 A Will you smoke less?
   B ....
3 A Did you stop smoking?
   B ....
4 A Are you going to stop smoking?
   B ....
5 A Did you have to stop smoking?
   B ....
6 A Did you have to smoke less?
   B ....

15 *At a Hotel*

Be sure not to miss the breakfast in an English hotel. If you are touring, you may not have to stop for lunch after a good English breakfast.

	(i)	(ii)	(iii)	(iv)
A	I wonder whether you have any vacancies for tonight.	Have you a single room for two nights?	Can I book a double room from now until Friday?	Have you got a twin-bedded room for one night?
B	Yes, I can offer you Room 24 on the first floor.[1]	Yes, but only on the top floor.	You can have Room 33, overlooking the sea.	I can let you have a room at the back.
A	How much is it?	What price is it?	What's the price?	What does it cost?
B	£2.90 a night excluding service.	£4.50 with service and TV.	£4.20 not counting the service.	With a private bath, £5.25, service included.
A	Can I see it, please?	Fair enough. Can you show me the room, please?	Can I have a look at it, please.	Can you show me something a little cheaper?
B	Certainly. Would you take a seat for a moment?	Of course. Would you like to follow me?	Yes, of course. Come this way.	Yes, of course. I won't keep you a moment.

[1] first floor: the floor above street level

1

Example

Can I reserve a double room from Sunday till Tuesday with a view of the sea?

1) ..... book ....?
2) .... private bathroom?
3) .... single ....?
4) .... now ....?
5) ..... have ....?

2

Example

STUDENT A Have you got **a double room**?
STUDENT B No, but I can let you have **two singles**.

1 A ..... a single room with a shower?
   B .... one with a bath.
2 A ..... a room overlooking the sea?
   B .... one facing the park.
3 A ..... a twin-bedded room?
   B .... one with a double bed.
4 A ..... two singles on the 2nd floor?
   B .... two on the top floor.
5 A ..... a double room from Monday to Friday?
   B .... one till Wednesday.

3◉

Reply to A's questions using the comparative form of the adjective.

Example

STUDENT A Is this **room big** enough for you, sir?
STUDENT B I suppose you haven't any-thing a little **bigger**, have you?

1 A ...... floor quiet ......?
   B

2 A ...... date early ......?
   B
3 A ...... room large ......?
   B
4 A ...... price reasonable ......?
   B
5 A ...... room comfortable ......?
   B

4

Reply to A's questions using 'something' plus an infinitive.

Example

STUDENT A **Are you hungry**?
STUDENT B Yes. Can you give **me** some-thing **to eat**?

1 A ...... the children restless?
   B .... something to play with?
2 A ...... she thirsty?
   B .... to drink?
3 A ...... you bored?
   B .... read?
4 A ... you waiting to sign the register?
   B .... to write with?
5 A ...... your bag broken?
   B .... to mend it with?

5*

You can say 'a room with a double bed' or 'a double-bedded room'.
Change A's sentences as in the example.

Example

STUDENT A I'd like a room with a double bed.
STUDENT B I'd like a double-bedded room.

1 A I want a room with twin beds.
   B ....
2 A This tip is for the waitress with the blue eyes.
   B ....
3 A Please reserve me a suite of two rooms.
   B ....
4 A I slept in the room with the red carpet.
   B ....
5 A I want to complain about the waiter with the long hair.
   B ....

Drills

16 *Finding a Room*

When inquiring about a room it is always a good idea to ask at the beginning whether laundry and heating are included in the price.

If you want to share a flat, look in the 'flats to let' column of an evening paper for advertisements like:

4th Girl shr. s/c H'stead flt. 01-134 2343 evenings.

This means that a fourth girl is required to share a self-contained flat in Hampstead, and that enquiries should be made by telephone in the evenings.

	(i)	(ii)	(iii)	(iv)
A	I believe you take in foreign students.	I've been told you might have a vacant room.	A friend told me I might find some accommodation here.	I wonder if you can help me – I'm looking for a room.
B	Yes, if you don't mind sharing.	Yes, I've got a spare single.	Yes, I'll have a room free after the weekend.	I have got a vacancy, yes.
A	How much is it?	What are your terms?	What's the price of the room?	What sort of price are you asking?
B	£9 per week including heating.	£3.50 for bed and breakfast.	£6.25 a week, but I can't do lunches.	£8.50 a week excluding laundry.
A	Do you think I could have a look at it, please?	Could I have a look at the room, please?	Do you mind if I come in?	Would it be convenient to see the room?
B	We're having it decorated at the moment. Will Friday do?[1]	It's a bit awkward just now. Could you come tomorrow?	Come in by all means, but it's in a terrible mess.	Can you call back later? We're right in the middle of lunch.

[1] will Friday do?: will Friday be all right?

1

Example

I wonder whether you could help me, I'm trying to find a family to live with.

1) . . . . looking for . . . .
2) . . . . a bed-sitting room.¹
3) . . . . can . . . .
4) . . . . if . . . .
5) . . . . somewhere to live.

2

Example

STUDENT A Would it be **convenient** to see the room now?

STUDENT B Can you **call back** later? I'm right in the middle of **lunch**.

1 A . . . . . . at all possible . . . . . .?
   B . . . . . . call again . . . . . . breakfast.
2 A . . . . . . all right . . . . . .?
   B . . . . come again . . . . . Woman's Hour.²
3 A . . . . . . in order . . . . . .?
   B . . . . . . look back . . . . . Coronation Street.³
4 A . . . . . . possible . . . . . .?
   B . . . . . . drop back . . . . . . a game of bridge.
5 A . . . . . . OK . . . . . .?
   B . . . . . . come round . . . . . . tea.

3

Example

STUDENT A When you say **£9**, is that with **lighting and heating**?

STUDENT B It's including **lighting** but excluding **heating**.

1 A . . . . . . £7.50 . . . . . . cleaning and bed linen?
   B . . . .

2 A . . . . . . £9.25 . . . . . . heating and laundry?
   B . . . .
3 A . . . . . . £7.00 . . . . . . lunch and supper?
   B . . . .
4 A . . . . . . £5.50 . . . . . . hot water and breakfast?
   B . . . .
5 A . . . . . . £10.00 . . . . . . all meals and heating?
   B . . . .

4 [⊚]

Example

STUDENT A Is it too **expensive** for you?
STUDENT B It ' is a bit **expensive**, yes.

1 A . . . . . . far . . . . . .?
   B . . . .
2 A . . . . . . cold . . . . . .?
   B . . . .
3 A . . . . . . small . . . . . .?
   B . . . .
4 A . . . . . noisy . . . . . .?
   B . . . .
5 A . . . . . dark . . . . . .?
   B . . . .

5 [⊚]

Respond to A's statements using a gerund after 'I don't mind'.

Example

STUDENT A You'll have to **share with somebody**, I'm afraid.

STUDENT B That's quite all right. I don't mind **sharing with somebody**.

1 A . . . . . do your own washing . . . . .
   B . . . .
2 A . . . . . . pay in advance . . . . . .
   B . . . .
3 A . . . . . . give me a deposit . . . . . .
   B . . . .
4 A . . . . cook your own breakfast . . . .
   B . . . .
5 A . . . . . . make your own bed . . . . .
   B . . . .

¹ a bed-sitting room: a one-roomed flat
² Woman's Hour: a BBC radio programme
³ Coronation Street: a popular television programme

17 *Making an Appointment*

Doctors often insist on appointments being made before they receive patients during the daily surgery hours.

	(i)	(ii)	(iii)	(iv)
A	Will Dr Black be able to see me at about 9.15 tomorrow?	I wonder whether the dentist could fit me in[1] early tomorrow?	I'd like to fix an appointment with the principal. Would nine tomorrow be all right?	Do you think the staff manager could see me tomorrow before 9.30?
B	Sorry, but he's fully booked till eleven unless there's a cancellation.	I'm afraid there's nothing before midday.	I'm afraid not. He's got rather a full day tomorrow.	He won't be in till 10.45, so the earliest would be 11.
A	Would ten to one be convenient?	How about 12.45?	Could I make it quarter to one?	Is 12.40 any good?
B	Yes, he's free then.	Sorry, but that's taken, too.	Sorry again, but I'll ring you if somebody cancels.	Yes, I'll make a note of it.

[1] fit me in: see me between his other engagements

I

Example

Will Dr Blackmore be able to fit me in at 4.30 tomorrow?

1) .... the dentist   ....?
2) .... see me ....?
3) ....three o'clock?
4) .... the manager   ....?
5) .... meet me ....?

2

Example

STUDENT A Can the **dentist** see me **today**?

STUDENT B No, I'm afraid not. **He** won't be **free** till **tomorrow**.

1 A .. the chief engineer .. on Friday?
    B ...... back ...... Tuesday.
2 A ... the manager ... before lunch?
    B ...... in ...... this afternoon.
3 A .... Miss Moore .... at three?
    B ...... ready ...... six.
4 A .... the Aliens' Officer .... now?
    B ...... available ...... 2.15.
5 A .... the doctor .... this week?
    B .... home ...... next month.

3

Example

STUDENT A Would it be convenient to see you **at 9.15**?

STUDENT B Do you think you could make it **9.30**?

1 A ...... after lunch?
    B ...... before lunch?

2 A ...:.. at eleven?
    B ...... a little later?
3 A ...... on Monday?
    B ...... on Wednesday?
4 A ...... at three o'clock?
    B ...... a bit earlier?
5 A .... some time on Friday morning?
    B ...... in the afternoon?

4[◎]

Example

STUDENT A **Monday**'s no good I'm afraid. He's **busy**.

STUDENT B How about **Tuesday**, then?

1 A 9.30 ...... engaged.
    B ...... 10.30 ......?
2 A The morning ...... out.
    B ...... the afternoon ......?
3 A Before lunch ...... not in.
    B ...... after lunch ......?
4 A The 15th ...... at a meeting.
    B ...... the 10th ......?
5 A The weekend ...... fully booked.
    B ...... mid-week ......?

5

Change A's sentences using a negative and 'unless'.

Example

STUDENT A You can see him if it's urgent.

STUDENT B You can't see him unless it's urgent.

1 A You can come earlier if he's free.
    B ....
2 A You can see him at 9 if he's in.
    B ....
3 A You can make it 9.30 if it's convenient for him.
    B ....
4 A You can have an appointment if somebody cancels.
    B ....
5 A You can see him now if it's important.
    B ....

18 Finding a Job

Normally the only jobs open to foreigners in the U.K. are in hotels and hospitals, or as domestic workers in schools or in families. A work permit is required for all jobs except 'au pair' positions. With the entry of Britain into the European Economic Community, the regulations changed and British Embassies abroad should be asked for the latest information.

	(i)	(ii)	(iii)	(iv)
A	Have you any vacancies for full-time staff?	I was wondering whether you needed any part-timers.	I'm looking for a job where I can live in.	Can you fix me up with a part-time job?
B	What did you have in mind?	What were you thinking of?	What exactly did you want?	Anything in particular that appeals to you?
A	Something in the domestic line.[1]	A hotel job of some sort.	I wouldn't mind[1] working in a pub.	I was rather hoping to find something in a school.
B	Have you had any experience?	Have you ever done anything similar?	Have you done anything like that before?	Have you done that kind of thing before?
A	No, I'm more or less straight from school.	Not so far, no.	Well, I once did a bit of waiting.	Yes, I was doing the same job last summer.
B	I can't promise anything, but I'll do my best.	There's nothing at present, but look back in a week.	Fill in this form and I'll let you know if anything turns up.	I might be able to help you, but I'd need references.

[1] in the domestic line: connected with domestic work

[1] I wouldn't mind: I would rather like

1

Example

There are no part-time vacancies at the moment but look back in a month.

1) . . . . call back . . . .
2) . . . . full-time . . . .
3) . . . . bar jobs . . . .
4) . . . . temporary . . . .
5) . . . . positions . . . .

2

Example

STUDENT A Have you any vacancies for **full-time chambermaids**?

STUDENT B No, but we need a **part-time waitress**.

1   A . . . . . . temporary cleaners?
   B . . . . . weekend barman.
2   A . . . . . . permanent waiters?
   B . . . . . night porter.
3   A . . . . . part-time washers-up?
   B . . . . . temporary gardener.
4   A . . . . . hospital porters?
   B . . . . . full-time cleaner.

3 ◉

Example

STUDENT A Is it a **full-time** job you're after?[1]

STUDENT B Actually, I was rather hoping to find something **part-time**.

1   A . . . . . . living-in[2] . . . . . .?
   B . . . . living-out.[3]

2   A . . . . . . au pair . . . . . .?
   B . . . . in a hotel.
3   A . . . . . . permanent . . . . . .?
   B . . . . temporary.
4   A . . . . . . outdoor . . . . . .?
   B . . . . indoors.
5   A . . . . . domestic . . . . . .?
   B . . . . secretarial.

4 ◉

Example

STUDENT A What sort of **occupation** did you have in mind?

STUDENT B I was thinking of something in the **hotel** line.

1   A . . . . . . job . . . . . .?
   B . . . . cleaning . . . .
2   A . . . . . work . . . . . .?
   B . . . . au pair . . . .
3   A . . . . . . post . . . . . .?
   B . . . . secretarial . . . .
4   A . . . . . position . . . . . .?
   B . . . . restaurant . . . .
5   A . . . . . employment . . . . . .?
   B . . . . catering . . . .

5 *◉

Reply to A's questions using the gerund.

Example

STUDENT A Does a **typist's** job appeal to you?

STUDENT B Yes, I've done quite a bit of **typing**.

1   A . . . . . . gardener's . . . . . .?
   B . . . .
2   A . . . . . . waiter's . . . . . .?
   B . . . .
3   A . . . . . . translator's . . . . . .?
   B . . . .
4   A . . . . . office cleaner's . . . . . .?
   B . . . .
5   A . . . . . fruit picker's . . . . . .?
   B . . . .

[1] you're after: you want
[2] a living-in job: a job providing a bedroom and meals
[3] a living-out job: a job not providing a bedroom and meals

19 At a Bank

Banks are open as follows:

9.30 – 3.30 Monday – Friday

Decimal Money System

Under this new system there are 100 new pence to one pound. The new coins are as follows:

Coppers	*Silver*
new halfpenny ($\frac{1}{2}$p)	five new pence (5p) – The old shilling
one new penny (1p)	ten new pence (10p) – The old two shillings
two new pence (2p)	fifty new pence (50p)

The old sixpence is still in circulation and is used as $2\frac{1}{2}$p. When there is no danger of confusion between old and new pence, the word 'new' is not used.

Bank notes remain at £1, £5, £10, and £20.

	(i)	(ii)	(iii)	(iv)
A	I'd like to change these marks, please.	Could you cash this travellers' cheque, please?	A new cheque book and these dollars into sterling, please.	Do you think you could change this note for me, please?
B	How do you want it?	How would you like it?	How did you want it?	How shall I give it to you?
A	It's all the same to me.	Five-pound notes, please.	Pound notes, please.	Notes and large silver, please.
B	Did you want anything else?	Anything else?	Do you want anything else?	Was there anything else?
A	Yes, I'd like to open a deposit account.[1]	Yes, I'm expecting some money from Paris. Is it in yet?	Yes, I'd like to know the rate for Swiss francs.	Yes, could you tell me my balance?[1]

[1] deposit account: an account with no cheque book

[1] balance: the amount of money in an account

1

Example

Would you tell me my balance and the current rate for dollars, please?

1) . . . . guilders . . . . . ?
2) . . . . give . . . . . statement[1] . . . .?
3) . . . . a new paying-in book . . . . . ?
4) Could . . . . ?

2

Example

I'd like to withdraw £15 from my deposit account, please.

1) . . . . current[2] . . . .
2) . . . . pay £125 into . . . .
3) . . . . our joint deposit account[3] . .
4) . . . . withdraw £40 from . . . .

3

Example

STUDENT A What do you need for your trip to **Frankfurt**?

STUDENT B Can you give me **£90** in **German marks**?

1   A . . . . Paris?
    B . . . . . . £40 . . . . French francs?
2   A . . . . Rome?
    B . . . . . . £80 . . . . Italian lire?
3   A . . . . New York?
    B . . . . . £100 . . . . American dollars?
4   A . . . . Amsterdam?
    B . . . . . . £70 . . . . Dutch guilders?
5   A . . . . Belgrade?
    B . . . . . . £50 . . . Yugoslav dinars?

4

Example

STUDENT A These **marks** are worth **£25**. How do you want it?

STUDENT B Two tens[4] and a five,[5] please.

1   A . . . . . francs . . . . . £16.50 . . . . .?
    B Two fives, six ones, and a fifty, please.
2   A . . . . . . dollars . . . . . . £28 . . . . . .?
    B A ten, two fives, and eight ones, please.
3   A . . . . . . lire . . . . . . £1.50 . . . . . .?
    B Three fifties, please.
4   A . . . . . krone . . . . . £19.50 . . . . .?
    B A ten, eight ones, and three fifties, please.
5   A . . . . . escudos . . . . . £10.15 . . . . .?
    B A ten, and three fives, please.

[1] statement: a detailed record of payments and withdrawals
[2] current account: an account with a cheque book
[3] joint account: an account shared with another person
[4] a ten: £10 or 10p according to the context
[5] a five: £5 or 5p according to the context

20 At a Barber's Shop

Barbers expect a tip of about 20 per cent on a normal haircut, but since most of them like to talk to their customers, the foreigner gets good value for his money in the form of twenty minutes' conversation practice.

	(i)	(ii)	(iii)	(iv)
A	How do you want it, sir?	How would you like it, sir?	How shall I cut it, sir?	How shall I do it, sir?
B	Just a trim,[1] please.	Not too much off, please.	Very short all over, please.	Just tidy it up a bit, please.
A	Would you like it washed?	How about a shampoo?	Shall I put some oil on?	Do you want some spray?
B	No, thank you. Just leave it as it is.	Not this time, thanks.	No, I don't think so, thanks.	No, nothing at all, thank you very much.

[1] a trim: when the barber does not cut off much hair

I

Example

Cut the sideboards fairly short, but leave the fringe as it is, please.

1)	.... top	.... sides		......
2)	.... back	.... front		......
3)	.... sides	.... top		......
4)	.... front	.... back and top		......
5)	.... fringe	.... sides		......

2

Example

Could you take a little more off the top, please?

1)	.... cut .... fringe ....?
2)	.... trim .... sides .....?
3)	.... take .... back .....?
4)	.... clip .... front .....?
5)	.... shave .... back.....?

3*◉

You can say: 'I'd like you to shampoo my hair' or 'I'd like my hair shampooed'.

Example

STUDENT A Do you want me to **shampoo your hair?**

STUDENT B Yes, I'd like **my hair shampooed.**

1	A	...... manicure your nails?
	B	....
2	A	...... trim your moustache?
	B	....
3	A	...... shave off your beard?
	B	....
4	A	...... move your parting?
	B	....
5	A	...... thin out the top?
	B	....

21 *Shopping*

Value Added Tax (VAT) was introduced in April 1973 to bring Britain into line with other countries in the European Economic Community.

	(i)	(ii)	(iii)	(iv)
A	Are you being served?	Is anybody looking after you?	Are you being attended to?	Are you being seen to?
B	No. What have you got in the way[1] of brown suede jackets, size 42?	No. I'm after a size 40 V-neck pullover in grey.	No. I'm trying to find a navy blue raincoat, size 42.	No. I'm looking for a pin-striped suit with a 34 waist.
A	Sorry, but we're sold right out.	The best I can do is a 36.	I can do the size, but not the colour.	I'm afraid I can't help you at the moment.
B	Are you likely to be getting any more in?	Could you order me one?	Do you think you could get one for me?	Will you be having any more in?
A	I should think so, yes. If you leave your phone number, I'll ring you.	I should imagine so, yes. If you leave your address, I'll contact you.	Yes, of course. Look in again Monday week.[1]	I doubt it, but you might be lucky at our High Street branch.

[1] in the way of brown suede jackets: in brown suede jackets

[1] Monday week: a week from next Monday

I

Example

I'm trying to find a navy blue raincoat in size 42.

1) . . . . blazer . . . .
2) . . . . 38.
3) I'm looking for . . . .
4) . . . . pullover . . . .
5) I'm after . . . .

2

Example

STUDENT A What have you got in the way of **white nylon shirts?**

STUDENT B Nothing in **nylon** at the moment, I'm afraid.

1 A . . . . brown suede shoes?
    B . . . . . . suede . . . . . .
2 A . . . . red leather handbags?
    B . . . . . . red . . . . . .
3 A . . . . plain silk ties?
    B . . . . . . silk . . . . . .
4 A . . . . black double-breasted jackets?
    B . . . . . . double-breasted . . . . . .
5 A . . . . light-weight navy blue blazers?
    B . . . . . . navy . . . . . .

3⊚

Reply to A's questions using the comparative form of the adjective.

Example

STUDENT A I'm sorry, but size **40** is the **biggest** I have in stock.

STUDENT B Are you likely to be having any **bigger** ones in?

---

1 A . . . . royal blue . . . . darkest . . . .
    B . . . . ?
2 A . . . . £3 . . . . . . cheapest . . . . . .
    B . . . . ?
3 A . . . . . . grey . . . . . lightest . . . . . .
    B . . . . ?
4 A . . . 31 inches . . . . . longest . . . . .
    B . . . . ?
5 A . . . . . . 15 . . . . . smallest . . . . . .
    B . . . . ?

4⊚

Reply to A's questions using 'more likely not to'.

Example

STUDENT A Are they likely **to have one in stock?**

STUDENT B They're more likely 'not **to have one in stock.**

1 A . . . be open during the lunch hour?
    B . . . .
2 A . . . . . . get them in by Tuesday?
    B . . . .
3 A . . . . . . change it for us?
    B . . . .
4 A . . . . . . give a guarantee?
    B . . . .
5 A . . . . . . accept a cheque?
    B . . . .

5*⊚

Reply to A's questions using the present continuous passive.

Example

STUDENT A Is anybody **serving** you?

STUDENT B Yes, I'm **being served**, thank you.

1 A . . . . . . looking after you?
    B . . . .
2 A . . . . . . attending to you?
    B . . . .
3 A . . . . . . seeing to you?
    B . . . .
4 A . . . . . . taking care of you?
    B . . . .

Drills

22 At a Theatre

It is not customary to tip the girl who shows you to your seat in a cinema or theatre.

	(i)	(ii)	(iii)	(iv)
A	I'd like to book two seats for tomorrow.	Can I still get tickets for tonight's show?	Are there any seats left for Saturday night?	Is it still possible to get tickets for tonight?
B	Would you like something in the front stalls?	The front row of the dress circle is fairly free.	A–11 and B–14 are all that's left.	You can sit wherever you like in the first row.
A	I suppose there's nothing further back, is there?	Are there any boxes?	Haven't you got anything cheaper?	Isn't there anything a little less dear?
B	Not unless you come to the matinée.[1]	No, I'm afraid that's all there is.	Only if somebody cancels.	No, I'm afraid you've left it rather late.

[1] matinée: afternoon show

Drills

1

Example

Are there any seats in the dress circle for Saturday's evening show?

1) . . . . upper circle . . . . ?
2) . . . . matinée?
3) Is there anything . . . . ?
4) . . . . tomorrow's . . . . . ?
5) . . . . rear stalls . . . . ?

2

Example

STUDENT A I suppose there's nothing in the **circle**, is there?

STUDENT B: I'm afraid not. Everything's booked except the **rear stalls**.

1 A . . . . . . front row . . . . . . ?
  B . . . . upper circle.
2 A . . . . . front stalls . . . . . . ?
  B . . . . four boxes.
3 A . . . . . third row . . . . . . ?
  B . . . . royal box.
4 A . . . . dress circle . . . . . . ?
  B . . . . back row.
5 A . . . . . upper circle . . . . . . ?
  B . . . . rear stalls.

3*

Reply to A's questions using the words 'whoever', 'whenever', 'wherever', 'whatever' or 'however'.

Example

STUDENT A **Which** programme can I take?

STUDENT B You can take **whichever** you like.

1 A Where can I sit?
  B . . . .
2 A What can I wear to the matinée?
  B . . . .
3 A How can I come?
  B . . . .
4 A Who can I bring with me?
  B . . . .
5 A When can I come?
  B . . . .

4*◉

Complete A's sentences by adding a question tag with a rising intonation. (You hope that the negative statement is not true.)

Example

STUDENT A **There's** nothing in the second row,

STUDENT B There's nothing in the second row, **is there?**

1 A You wouldn't like the third row,
  B . . . . ?
2 A You never get cancellations,
  B . . . . ?
3 A You haven't anything cheaper,
  B . . . . ?
4 A There weren't any tickets left,
  B . . . . ?
5 A There's no chance of a box,
  B . . . . ?

5*◉

Complete A's sentences by adding a question tag with a falling intonation. (You expect that the statement is true.)

Example

STUDENT A **The matinee doesn't** start till 2.30,

STUDENT B The matinée doesn't start till 2.30, **does it?**

1 A I can sit wherever I like,
  B . . . . ?
2 A He usually sits in the circle,
  B . . . . ?
3 A You booked the seats,
  B . . . . ?
4 A There isn't a performance on Sunday,
  B . . . . ?
5 A The tickets came to £2.50,
  B . . . . ?

23 Police Registration

Regulations for entry into the U.K. are strict, and officers have the power to refuse entry to anybody not having the correct papers and enough money to support himself. British Embassies are able to give the latest information to anybody planning a long visit.

	(i)	(ii)	(iii)	(iv)
A	I've come along to register with you.	I was told to report to the Aliens' Officer.[1]	I've come to see you about my registration.	I understand I'm supposed to register.
B	Has your passport been up to the Home Office?[1]	Has your permission to stay been extended?	Has the school sent your passport up to London?	Has your employer arranged for an extension?[1]
A	Yes, they granted me three months.	Yes, I'm all right until July.	Yes, I've got until the end of the year.	Yes, I've been given three months.
B	I'd like your address in this country, please.	I shall have to see your work permit as well, please.	Then I'll need two photographs, and 25p, please.	Can I see your registration book, please?

[1] Home Office: the government department called 'The Ministry of the Interior' in most countries

[1] Aliens' Officer: the officer in police stations responsible for foreigners

[1] an extension: an extension of permission to stay in the U.K.

I

Example

I've come along to advise you about my change of address.

1) . . . . school.
2) . . . . inform . . . .
3) . . . . new au pair job.
4) . . . . ask . . . .
5) . . . . registration book.

2

Example

STUDENT A Do I have to **register with the police?**

STUDENT B Yes, you're supposed to **register at once.**

1 A . . . . declare these cigarettes?
  B . . . . . . declare everything.

2 A . . . . report my cnange of address?
  B . . . . report every time you move.

3 A . . . . attend school?
  B . . . . . . attend for 15 hours a week.

4 A . . . . produce a bank statement?
  B . . . prove you have enough money.

5 A . . . . take a driving test?
  B . . . . . . take one within a year.

3*

Reply to A's questions using the correct form of the passive and the word 'three'.

Example

STUDENT A **They[1] gave me** an extension of six months.

STUDENT B [1]**I was only given** three.

1 A They've given me . . . . . .
  B . . . .

2 A They'll give me . . . . . .
  B . . . .

3 A They'd given me . . . . . .
  B . . . .

4 A They'd give me . . . . . .
  B . . . .

5 A They're going to give me . . . . . .
  B . . . .

6 A They give me . . . . . .
  B . . . .

7 A They're giving me . . . . . .
  B . . . .

they: the officials at the Home Office

24 Asking for Change

Shops near telephone boxes are always being asked for change, and usually refuse to give it. If you need change urgently, and cannot find anybody to help you, it is a good idea to buy a small item, such as a box of matches, and ask for your change to include the required coins.

	(i)	(ii)	(iii)	(iv)
A	Excuse me, but could I trouble you for some change?	Sorry to trouble you, but have you change for a 50?	Excuse me. I wonder whether you could change 50p?	Excuse me. Could you oblige me with some change?
B	Let me see. Do you want coppers or silver?	I'll have a look. What do you want it for?	Let's see. Coppers or silver?	I'll see what I've got. What's it for?
A	I want to make a trunk-call.[1]	I have to get a book of stamps.	It's for a long-distance call.	I need some cigarettes from this machine.
B	You'd better have silver, then.	In that case you need silver.	Will tens do?	I can let you have some tens, if that's any good.

[1] trunk call: long-distance telephone call

48

Drills

I

Example

I can let you have some fifties if that's any good.

1) .... fives ....
2) .... help.
3) ..... give you ....
4) .... tens ....
5) .... use.

2

Example

STUDENT A Excuse me. Have you got **any coppers**?

STUDENT B I'm afraid not. Will **silver** do?

1 A ...... a pound note?
   B ...... two fifties ......?
2 A ...... any fives?
   B ...... tens ......?
3 A ...... any coffee?
   B ...... tea ......?
4 A ...... any French cigarettes?
   B ..... American ......?
5 A ...... any two pence pieces?
   B ...... pennies ......?

3⊚

You can say 'Why do you need it?' or 'What do you need it for?' Change A's questions by using 'What ...... for?'

Example

STUDENT A Why do you want it?

STUDENT B What do you want it for?

1 A Why are you crying?
   B ....?
2 A Why have you come?
   B ....?
3 A Why did you choose it?
   B ....?
4 A Why are we waiting?
   B ....?
5 A Why do you want to see it?
   B ....?

25 Telephoning (1)

Shops and restaurants do not allow customers to use their office telephones, but some have telephone boxes and there are boxes in the street and in public buildings.

When giving numbers to an operator, read each figure separately. Zero is read as the letter 'O'. When the same figures occur together, the word 'double' is used. 886103 is read as 'double eight six one O three'.

Some of the telephone services available are:

Emergency calls to the Fire Brigade, Police, and Ambulance Service, for which you should dial 999.

A.D.C., which stands for 'advise duration and charge', means that when the call is finished the operator rings you back to tell you how long the call was and how much it cost. Directory Enquiries give information about numbers both in the U.K. and abroad. Personal calls are made to a particular person. A fixed charge is made for the service, but you do not pay for the time taken to find the person. If he is not there the call is tried again later without further charge. Transferred-charge calls are paid for by the person receiving the call rather than the caller.

	(i)	(ii)	(iii)	(iv)
A	Number please.	Number please.	Number please.	Number please.
B	I'd like to make an A.D.C., personal call to 01-486-2435, please.	Eastbourne 74655, personal with A.D.C., please.	Could you get me Luton 12507? Make it personal, please.	Can I have a personal call to Bedford 645932, please?
A	What is the name of the person you wish to speak to?	Who do you want to speak to?	The name of the person you are calling, please?	Who are you calling?
B	Miss Susan Greene. G-R double E-N-E.	Extension 214.	The Export Manager.	I'm not sure of the name, but it's room 211.
A	What is your number, please?	What number are you calling from?	Where are you calling from?	Your exchange and number, please?
B	Brighton 11865.	Aberdeen 605.	Belfast 74520.	Swansea 66932.

1

Example

Would you get me a transferred-charge call to Eastbourne 74655, please?

1) I'd like to make ....

2) .... an A.D.C. personal call ....

3) .... to 01-347-6654 .....

4) Could I have ....?

5) .... an A.D.C. call ....?

2

Example

STUDENT A Is that **Eastbourne 69523**?

STUDENT B No, you've got the wrong number. This is **Eastbourne 65932**.

1 A ...... The Army and Navy Stores?
   B ...... The Battersea Dogs' Home.

2 A ...... extension 319?
   B ...... extension 913.

3 A ...... Polegate 4378?
   B ...... Burwash 4378.

4 A ...... Continental?[1]
   B ...... Telegrams.

5 A ...... Directory Enquiries?
   B ...... International.[2]

3◉

Example

STUDENT A Did you say **Foster: F-O-S-T-E-R**?

STUDENT B No, I said **Gloucester: G-L-O-U-C-E-S-T-E-R**.

1 A ...... chicken ......?
   B ...... kitchen ......

2 A ...... Midwood ......?
   B ...... Bradford ......

3 A ...... Turkey ......?
   B ...... Torquay ......

4 A ...... expect ......?
   B ...... except ......

5 A ...... Chertsey ......?
   B ...... Jersey ......

4*◉

Make questions from A's statements by using 'what', 'who' or 'where'.

Example

STUDENT A They're looking at **something**.

STUDENT B **What** are they looking at?

1 A They're thinking of somebody.
   B ....?

2 A They're apologising about something.
   B ....?

3 A They're calling from somewhere.
   B ....?

4 A They're talking to somebody.
   B ....?

5 A They're looking for something.
   B ....?

[1] Continental: the Continental Exchange
[2] International: the International Exchange

26 Telephoning (2)

In business, telephones are answered by giving the name of the firm. Private telephones are normally answered by giving the number only.

	(i)	(ii)	(iii)	(iv)
A	Eastbourne 54655.	486-4459.	Blackpool 15014.	922-6530.
B	Hallo. John here. Can I speak to Mary, please?	Hallo. David Black speaking. May I have a word with June?[1]	Hallo. This is James here. Is Alice there, please?	Hallo. My name's Frank Duncan. Could I talk to Linda, please?
A	Hold the line, please.[1]	I'll just see if she's in.	Hang on a moment.[1]	I'll find out if she's at home.
B	OK.	Right you are.	All right.	Right.
A	Sorry, but she's out.	I'm afraid she's not here.	I think she's gone shopping.	Sorry, but she won't be back till Monday.
B	Would you tell her I rang?	Could you take a message?	Would you ask her to call back?	Can you tell her to ring me when she gets back?
A	I'd be glad to.	Yes, of course.	Certainly.	With pleasure.

[1] hold the line:. wait (used only on the telephone)

[1] May I have a word with June?: May I have a short conversation with June?

[1] hang on: wait

1

Example

I'll just find out if Dr Armstrong's at home.

1) ...... inquire ....
2) .... Richard's ....
3) .... ready.
4) .... the coat's ....
5) ...... see ....

2

Example

STUDENT A Can I **speak to Dick**, please?

STUDENT B I'm afraid **he** won't be **here** till **tea-time**.

I A ...... talk to your mother ....?
  B ...... in ...... later.
2 A ...... have a word with Joe ....?
  B ..... home ...... tomorrow.
3 A ..... speak to the foreman ....?
  B ..... available ..... after lunch.
4 A ...... have a word with Nurse Evans ....?
  B ...... on duty ...... tonight.
5 A ..... talk to the manageress ....?
  B ..... free ...... 7.30.

3

Example

STUDENT A Hallo. Is **Alice** there, please?

STUDENT B Sorry, **she's** out. Shall I ask **her** to ring you when **she** gets in?

I A ...... your parents ......?
  B ....?
2 A ...... Major Carson ......?
  B ....?
3 A ..... your sister ......?
  B ....?
4 A ...... Henry ......?
  B ....?

4

Reply to A's questions using the Present Perfect Tense.

Example

STUDENT A When's **he going**?

STUDENT B I think **he's** already **gone**.

I A When are they leaving?
  B ....
2 A When's Peter phoning?
  B ....
3 A When's she having lunch?
  B ....
4 A When are they coming back?
  B ....
5 A When's Jack ringing?
  B ....

27 In a Post Office

As well as the main post offices in town centres, there are numerous sub-post offices in suburbs and villages. These are often inside grocers' shops or general stores. Post offices also offer a form of banking service known as the 'Post Office Savings Bank'. This is useful, as money may be withdrawn from any post office in the U.K. on production of a special savings book. One way of sending money through the post inside the U.K. is to buy postal orders which may be cashed at any of the post offices in the country. Registered envelopes for valuable items such as money and passports are also on sale.

	(i)	(ii)	(iii)	(iv)
A	What's the postage on these letters to Thailand, please?	Could you tell me how much this parcel to France is?	How much is this greetings telegram[1] to Germany, please?	What's the surcharge on this express letter, please?
B	I'll have to check. Do you need anything else?	I think I'd better look that up. Was there anything else?	I'll just make sure. Anything else?	I'll have a look. Did you want anything else?
A	Yes. A 3p stamp, please.	Yes. A postal order for 25p and an air letter form.	Yes. Half a dozen air mail labels and a book of stamps.	Yes. While I'm about it,[1] I'll have a large registered envelope.
B	That'll be 85p in all.	87p, please.	75p exactly, please.	That comes to 90p.

[1] a greetings telegram: a telegram on a decorated form for birthdays etc.

[1] While I'm about it: While I'm buying things in this post office

54

1

Example

What's the postage on this letter to Bangkok, please?

1) . . . . parcel . . . .?
2) . . . . Lisbon . . . .?
3) How much is it for . . . .?
4) . . . . card . . . .?
5) . . . . cable . . . .?

2

Example

STUDENT A Do you think I ought to **write**?

STUDENT B No, I think you'd better **phone**.

1 A . . . . . . post it?
   B . . . . . . take it yourself.
2 A . . . . . . send him a card?
   B . . . . . . write a letter.
3 A . . . . . . pay by cheque?
   B . . . . . send a postal order.
4 A . . . . . . write a birthday card?
   B . . . . . send a greetings telegram.
5 A . . . . . . cable him?
   B . . . . . . ring him up.

3*◉

Make questions from A's statements using 'anything else', 'anyone else' or 'anywhere else'.

Example

STUDENT A I rang the butcher.

STUDENT B Did you ring **anyone else**?

1 A I went to London.
   B . . . .?
2 A I bought some stamps.
   B . . . .?
3 A I wrote to Tom.
   B . . . .?
4 A I posted the cards.
   B . . . .?
5 A I phoned the manager.
   B . . . .?

Drills

28 *Asking about Health*

When an Englishman asks you about your health, he is probably only doing so out of politeness. Unless he knows you have been ill, he is certainly not expecting a detailed medical report, and will be most surprised if you give him one.

	(i)	(ii)	(iii)	(iv)
A	How's your father keeping?	Where's Tony this evening?	How's your brother these days?	I haven't seen Bob lately. How is he?
B	He's been off work for a day or two.	He's not feeling very well.	He hasn't been too well just recently.	As a matter of fact, he's laid up.[1]
A	What's wrong with him?	Really? What's the trouble?	I'm sorry to hear that. What's the matter?	Oh dear! What's up with him?
B	He's gone down with a cold.	I think he must have eaten something.	I think he's been over-working.	We don't know, but we're having the doctor in to-morrow.
A	Tell him I hope he soon feels better.	Give him my regards and tell him to take things easy.	I hope he soon gets over it.	Let me know if there's anything I can do.
B	That's very kind of you. I'll pass it on.	Thank you very much. I'll tell him what you said.	Thank you. He'll be pleased to hear you asked after him.	Thanks very much. I'll tell him you inquired about him.

[1]laid up: ill

I

Example
   Give Tony my best wishes and tell him not to overdo things.
1) . . . . regards . . . .
2) . . . . overwork.
3) . . . . to get well soon.
4) . . . . to take things easy.
5) . . . . Roger . . . .

2⊚

Example
STUDENT A **Peter**'s not feeling very well.
STUDENT B I'm sorry to hear that. Tell
   him I hope **he** soon feels better.

1   A   Brenda . . . .
    B   . . . .
2   A   The children . . . .
    B   . . . .
3   A   Henry . . . .
    B   . . . .
    The girls . . . .
        . . . .
        . . . .

3⊚

Example
STUDENT A I haven't seen **Bob** for some
   time. How is **he**?
STUDENT B As a matter of fact, **he** hasn't
   been too well just lately.

1   A   . . . . . . your sister . . . . . .?
    B   . . . .
2   A   . . . . . . Professor White . . . . . .?
    B   . . . .
3   A   . . . . . Tom . . . . . .?
    B   . . . .
4   A   . . . . . . you . . . . . .?
    B   . . . .
5   A   . . . . . . the Robinsons . . . . . .?
    B   . . . .

4*⊚

Reply to A's questions using the phrase
'must have' plus the past participle of the
verb.

Example
STUDENT A Are you sure **he knew**?
STUDENT B Yes, **he 'must have known.**

1   A   . . . . she ate it?
    B   . . . .
2   A   . . . . they took it?
    B   . . . .
3   A   . . . . you did it?
    B   . . . .
4   A   . . . . he understood?
    B   . . . .
5   A   . . . . she broke it?
    B   . . . .

29 At a Doctor's Surgery

Foreigners taken ill or involved in accidents while in the U.K. are entitled to free medical treatment under the British National Health Service.

	(i)	(ii)	(iii)	(iv)
A	I've got a sore throat and my chest hurts.	I feel shivery and I've got a pain in my stomach.	I keep feeling dizzy, and I've got a headache.	I'm running a temperature, and I feel sick.
B	How long have you been like this?	How long have you had it?	How long has this been going on?	Since when have you been feeling like this?
A	Two or three days now.	The best part of a week.[1]	It came on yesterday.	It all started the day before yesterday.
B	I should think you've got flu: there's a lot of it about.	By the sound of it, you've caught a chill.	I should say you're generally run down.[1]	You seem to have picked up some sort of infection.
A	What do you advise?	What should I do?	What ought I to do?	What do you think I should do?
B	Take this prescription to the chemist's and then go straight to bed.	I'll give you something for it, and come to see you in a couple of days.	It's nothing serious, but you'd better stay in bed for a day or two.	Stay away from work till Monday, and don't overdo things.

[1] the best part of a week: most of a week

[1] run down: in poor health due to tiredness and overwork

I

Example

I've got a temperature and I feel shivery.

1) . . . . sore throat . . . .
2) . . . . dizzy.
3) . . . . headache . . . .
4) . . . . sick.
5) . . . . chill . . . .

2◉

Example

STUDENT A Have you got **a headache**?
STUDENT B No, I keep feeling **dizzy**.

1   A . . . . . . a cold?
    B . . . . sick.
2   A . . . . . . a cough?
    B . . . . hot and cold.
3   A . . . . . . a temperature?
    B . . . . faint.
4   A . . . . . . a pain?
    B . . . . weak.
5   A . . . . . . a sore throat?
    B . . . . shivery.

3

You can say 'very nearly a month' or 'the best part of a month'. Change A's statements by using the phrase 'the best part of . . . . . . '.

Example

STUDENT A I've been ill **for very nearly a month**.

STUDENT B I've been ill **for the best part of a month**.

1   A He's been running a temperature for very nearly a week.
    B . . . .

2   A The doctor's fees were very nearly £20.
    B . . . .

3   A She was in hospital for very nearly a year.
    B . . . .

4   A My operation lasted for very nearly two hours.
    B . . . .

4

You can say 'a pain in my ear' or 'ear-ache'. Change A's statements in a similar way.

Example

STUDENT A I've got **a pain in my ear**.
STUDENT B I've got **ear-ache**.

1   A . . . . . . tooth.
    B . . . .
2   A . . . . . . stomach.
    B . . . .
3   A . . . . . . back
    B . . . .
4   A . . . . . . head.
    B . . . . a . . . .

5*

You can say 'it looks as if . . . . . .' or 'by the look of it . . . . . .'. Change A's statements in a similar way, altering the verb to the corresponding noun.

Example

STUDENT A **It looks as if** it's **tonsillitis**.
STUDENT B **By the look of it**, it's **tonsillitis**.

1   A It feels as if it's broken.
    B . . . .
2   A It smells as if it's cough mixture.
    B . . . .
3   A It sounds as if it's bronchitis.
    B . . . .
4   A It tastes as if it's aspirin.
    B . . . .
5   A It looks as if it's mumps.
    B . . . .

30 At a Chemist's Shop

It is possible to obtain emergency medicines from certain chemists after normal shopping hours. If the shop is closed look in the window for the list of chemists who are open late on that particular day. A fixed charge is made by the chemist is made by the chemist in respect of each prescription: at present, this amounts to 20 pence regardless of the value of the medicine. If you regularly take a certain drug, it is as well to remember that it may not be available in the U.K. except with a doctor's prescription. Chemists in the U.K. sell cosmetics and toilet preparations as well as photographic supplies. Films may be left at a chemist's shop for developing.

	(i)	(ii)	(iii)	(iv)
A	The doctor's given me this prescription.	Could you make up this prescription for me, please?	I've just been given this prescription by Dr Worrall.	Can I leave this prescription with you?
B	It'll only take five minutes, so perhaps you'll wait.	I'll do it for you straight away.	You can call back for it in about an hour.	I'll have it ready for you by 5.30.
A	Have you also got something suitable for sore lips?	By the way, what do you suggest for sunburn?	Can you also give me something for this rash?[1]	I'd like something for a stye,[1] too.
B	Rub in this cream every four hours.	This ointment should clear up the trouble.	Try this tube of jelly.	Put this lotion on three times a day.

[1] a rash: a skin irritation

[1] a stye: a spot on the eye-lid

1

Example

Can you give me something to clear up a rash?

1) . . . . a cough?
2) . . . . relieve . . . . . . ?
3) . . . . . . sell . . . . ?
4) . . . . a headache?
5) . . . . soothe sore lips?

2⦿

Example

STUDENT A What do you suggest for **sunburn?**

STUDENT B Try **this cream.** I think you'll find **it**'ll do the trick.[1]

1 A . . . . indigestion?
  B . . . . . . these tablets . . . . . .
2 A . . . . insomnia?
  B . . . . . . these pills . . . . . .
3 A . . . . a sore throat?
  B . . . . this gargle . . . . . .
4 A . . . . an upset stomach?
  B . . . . . this mixture . . . . . .
5 A . . . . dandruff?
  B . . . . this shampoo . . . . . .

3⦿

Example

STUDENT A Here's some **mixture** for you to **drink.**

STUDENT B How often am I supposed to **drink** it?

1 A . . . . . . pills . . . . . . swallow.
  B . . . . ?
2 A . . . . . . ointment . . . . . . apply.
  B . . . . ?
3 A . . . . . . lotion . . . . . . put on.
  B . . . . ?
4 A . . . . . . tablets . . . . . . take.
  B . . . . ?
5 A . . . . . . gargle . . . . . . use.
  B . . . . ?

4*

Respond to A's statements using the passive and the word 'cream'.

Example

STUDENT A The chemist **gave** me ointment.

STUDENT B 'I **was given** cream.

1 A The chemist's giving me ointment.
  B . . . .
2 A The chemist'll give me ointment.
  B . . . .
3 A The chemist's given me ointment.
  B . . . .
4 A The chemist gives me ointment.
  B . . . .
5 A The chemist was giving me ointment.
  B . . . .
6 A The chemist'd give me ointment.
  B . . . .
7 A The chemist'd given me ointment.
  B . . . .

[1] do the trick: solve the problem

31 Meeting People after a Long Time

Although handshakes are not often given by the English, it is quite common to shake hands when meeting a friend one has not seen for six months or so.

	(i)	(ii)	(iii)	(iv)
A	We haven't seen you for ages. Have you been ill?	How nice to see you again. Where have you been? Home?	Come in and sit down. We haven't seen much of you lately.	You're quite a stranger.[1] Have you moved or something?
B	No, I've been up north for a month.	No, I've been visiting relations.	No, I've been away on holiday.	No, I've had a few weeks in Scotland.
A	Where was that?	Whereabouts?	Where exactly?	Where did you go?
B	Glasgow. I got back the day before yesterday.	I went to Stirling to see an uncle of mine.	Edinburgh. I've got a cousin there.	Aberdeen. I stayed with my brother.

[1] you're quite a stranger: I haven't seen you for a long time

I

Example

Mrs Hughes must have gone to her mother's. I haven't seen her for a fortnight.

1) Dave .... back to Sydney .... since Easter.
2) They .... shopping .... for an hour.
3) Brian .... to work .... since 8.30.
4) She .... abroad .... for weeks.
5) The Smiths .... on holiday .... since July.

2

Example

STUDENT A I didn't see **you** last week. Where were **you**?
STUDENT B I went **up to London** to visit a friend of **mine**.

1 A ..... him .....?
   B ..... over to Paris .....
2 A ..... your mother-in-law .....?
   B ..... down to Bournemouth .....
3 A ..... the children .....?
   B ..... across to Dieppe .....
4 A ..... you and Jackie .....?
   B ..... to Ramsgate .....
5 A ..... Tony .....?
   B ..... over to Dublin .....

3

Example

STUDENT A Where's **the landlady**?
STUDENT B I don't know. I haven't seen **her** for **ages**.

1 A ..... Mike and Tim?
   B .... weeks.
2 A ..... my slide-rule?
   B .... days.
3 A ..... Mrs Maggs?
   B .... some time.
4 A ..... the people downstairs?
   B .... quite a while.

4

Example

STUDENT A Where's **Stuart**?
STUDENT B I really couldn't say. I haven't seen **him** since **Thursday**.

1 A ..... Herbert and Rose?
   B .... Easter.
2 A ..... the tea-pot?
   B .... breakfast.
3 A ..... Cinderella?
   B .... midnight.
4 A ..... my hot water bottle?
   B .... last night.
5 A ..... the Fosters?
   B .... November.

5*

Reply to A's questions using 'since' or 'for' where required.

Example

STUDENT A Where's **Sue**?
STUDENT B I'm afraid I don't know. I haven't seen **her** since **11.30**.

1 A ..... the sugar?
   B .... breakfast.
2 A ..... my football boots?
   B .... over a week.
3 A ..... Professor Watson?
   B .... April.
4 A ..... his wife?
   B .... six weeks.
5 A ..... the Smiths?
   B .... ages.

32 Introductions and Opening Conversation Gambits

A man is introduced to a woman, unless he is much older and more senior. Young men are introduced to older men, and young women to older women.

	(i)	(ii)	(iii)	(iv)
A	Wendy, I'd like you to meet my brother, Sam.	Mrs Hughes, this is Peter Brown.	Mother, this is Joe's brother, David.	Mrs Stacey, I'd like to introduce my Greek friend, Milos.
B	How do you do?	How do you do?	How do you do?	How do you do?
C	How do you do?	How do you do?	How do you do?	How do you do?
B	What do you think of life in England?	How do you find things over here?	How do you like London?	What are your first impressions of England?
C	I'm still feeling pretty homesick.	If it wasn't for the climate, I'd like it very much.	It's quite different from what I expected.	Of course, it's much colder here than it is at home.
B	It's bound to[1] be strange at first.	It won't take you long to settle down.	Don't worry; you'll soon get used to it.	Never mind; you'll be all right in a week or two.

[1] bound to: sure to

1

Example

Mrs James, I'd like to introduce my brother, Pat.

1) . . . . sister . . .
2) . . . . you to meet . . . .
3) Miss Brown, ...
4) . . . . this is . . . .
5) . . . . my brother-in-law, Joe.

2

Example

STUDENT A Don't you find English **meals** strange?

STUDENT B Yes, I can't get used to the way you **call 'lunch' 'dinner'**.

1 A . . . . . . houses . . . . . .?
  B . . . . leave the bedrooms unheated.
2 A . . . . . . food . . . . . .?
  B . . . . cook fruit.
3 A . . . . . . conversation . . . . . .?
  B . . . . always talk about the weather.
4 A . . . . . . beer . . . . . .?
  B . . . . drink it warm.
5 A . . . . . . people . . . . . .?
  B . . . . don't talk at breakfast.

3

Example

STUDENT A How do you find things in **England**?

STUDENT B If it wasn't for the **climate** I'd like it very much.

1 A . . . . in your new job?
  B . . . . . . hours . . . . . .
2 A . . . . in your new class?
  B . . . . . . teacher . . . . . .
3 A . . . . in your new family?
  B . . . . . children . . . . . .
4 A . . . . in London?
  B . . . . . the traffic . . . . . .
5 A . . . . in your new flat?
  B . . . . . the neighbours . . . . . .

4

Example

STUDENT A When **will it be ready**?
STUDENT B **It'll be ready** in a **day** or two.

1 A When's he coming back?
  B . . . . . . week . . . . . .
2 A When will it be finished?
  B . . . . . . year . . . . . .
3 A When are you leaving?
  B . . . . . . hour . . . . . .
4 A When will she be going back?
  B . . . . . . month . . . . . .

5⊙

Respond to A's statements using the phrase 'bound to'.

Example

STUDENT A **I'm still feeling pretty home-sick.**

STUDENT B **You're** bound to feel **home-sick** at first.

1 A He . . . . . . miserable.
  B . . . .
2 A They . . . . . . depressed.
  B . . . .
3 A She . . . . . . upset.
  B . . . .
4 A We . . . . . . bewildered.
  B . . . .
5 A I . . . . . . lonely.
  B . . . .

33 Christmas, New Year and Easter Greetings

Public holidays in the U.K. are known as Bank Holidays and are as follows: New Year's Day, Good Friday, Easter Monday, the last Monday in May or the first Monday in June, the last Monday in August or the first Monday in September, Christmas Day and Boxing Day (the day after Christmas Day).

(i)

A Happy Christmas!

B Thanks very much. Same to you!

A Are you doing anything special?

B We're having some friends round. What're you doing?

A I daresay I'll just take things easy.

(ii)

Happy Easter!

Thanks. And you, too!

Are you doing anything?

I've been invited over to Pat's. And you?

My room-mate's[1] giving a party.

(iii)

Happy New Year!

Thank you very much. You, too!

Are you going anywhere?

I thought about going to my sister's. How about you?

I'll probably just stay at home.

(iv)

Have a good weekend.

Thanks. The same to you!

Have you got anything planned?

I can't afford to do much. What about you?

I expect I'll stay with my family.

[1] room-mate: the person I share my room with

I

Example

I can't afford to go anywhere over the Bank Holiday; I'll just stay at home.

1) . . . . Christmas   . . . .
2) . . . . do much . . . .
3) . . . . here.
4) . . . . Easter   . . . .
5) . . . . go away . . . .

2[◉]

Respond to A's greetings.

Example

STUDENT A **Happy New Year**!
STUDENT B Thanks very much. **Happy New Year** to 'you, too.

1   A   Happy Christmas!
    B   . . . .
2   A   Happy Easter!
    B   . . . .
3   A   Merry Christmas!
    B   . . . .
4   A   A very Happy New Year!
    B   . . . .

3

Respond to A's good wishes.

Example

STUDENT A Have a good **weekend**!
STUDENT B Thanks. Same to you.

1   A   . . . . Christmas!
    B   . . . .

2   A   . . . . Easter!
    B   . . . .
3   A   . . . . time!
    B   . . . .
4   A   . . . . Whitsun!
    B   . . . .
5   A   . . . . holiday!
    B   . . . .

4^{*◉}

Reply to A's questions using 'at' or 'to'.

Example

STUDENT A Where's **Dave**?
STUDENT B He's at **his** sister's.
STUDENT A Where's **Dave** going?
STUDENT B He's going to **his** sister's.

1   A   Where's Mary gone?
    B   . . . .
2   A   Where's Mary?
    B   . . . .
3   A   Where will they go?
    B   . . . .
4   A   Where was he?
    B   . . . .
5   A   Where have I got to go?
    B   . . . .

5[*]

Respond to A's statements using a negative question in the passive.

Example

STUDENT A Pat's **invited** me for Boxing Day.
STUDENT B **Haven't 'I been invited**, too?

1   A   Pat invited me for Boxing Day.
    B   . . . . ?
2   A   Pat'll invite me for Boxing Day.
    B   . . . . ?
3   A   Pat's inviting me for Boxing Day.
    B   . . . . ?
4   A   Pat was inviting me for Boxing Day.
    B   . . . . ?
5   A   Pat ought to invite me for Boxing Day.
    B   . . . . ?

34 *Saying Good-bye*

For the English, 'keeping in touch' usually means nothing more than sending a Christmas card. The average English family receives large numbers of cards, which are displayed in the living-room for all to see. Your English friends will be delighted if you remember them with a card at Christmas.

	(i)	(ii)	(iii)	(iv)
A	I've come to say good-bye.	I'd like to say good-bye to you all.	I'm ringing to say good-bye.	I've just called in to say good-bye.
B	When are you off?[1]	What time are you going?	When are you setting off?	What time are you leaving?
A	I'm flying home on Sunday.	My train leaves at 7.25.	I'm catching the 11.35 boat.	I'm going to try to get away by ten.
B	Good-bye then, and all the very best.	Well, good-bye, and have a good journey.	Cheerio then, and don't forget to keep in touch.	Good-bye then, and remember me to your parents.
A	Cheerio. Say good-bye to the rest of the family for me, won't you?	Good-bye. Remember to look me up[1] if ever you're in Rome.	Good-bye, and thanks for everything.	Good-bye. See you next year.

[1] off: going

[1] look me up: this means 'come to see me' and not 'stay with me'

1

Example
Don't forget to give us a ring if ever you're in London.

1) . . . . our way.
2) . . . . drop us a line¹ . . . .
3) . . . . in town.
4) . . . . look us up . . . .
5) Be sure . . . .

2

Example
STUDENT A When are you off?
STUDENT B My **ship sails at 5.30.**
STUDENT A I hope you have a good **voyage.**

1 A . . . . ?
   B . . . . bus leaves at nine o'clock.
   A . . . . journey.
2 A . . . . ?
   B . . . . plane takes off at 21.40.
   A . . . . flight.
3 A . . . . ?
   B . . . . train goes at 4.15.
   A . . . . journey.
4 A . . . . ?
   B . . . . ferry leaves at 11.35.
   A . . . . crossing.
5 A . . . . ?
   B . . . . coach goes at midday.
   A . . . . trip.

3

Example
STUDENT A Good-bye and thank you very much for **all you've done.**
STUDENT B It was a pleasure. Hope to see you again **next year.**

1 A . . . . . a wonderful time.
   B . . . . . in the spring.
2 A . . . . . everything.
   B . . . . . some day.
3 A . . . . . all your help.
   B . . . . . next time you're here.
4 A . . . . . showing me around.
   B . . . . . next summer.

4◉

Example
STUDENT A Remember me to **your parents,** won't you?
STUDENT B Yes, I'll give **them** your regards as soon as I get back.

1 A . . . . . . David . . . . . . ?
   B . . . .
2 A . . . . . . your mother . . . . ?
   B . . . .
3 A . . . . . . the children . . . . . . ?
   B . . . .
4 A . . . . . . your father . . . . . . ?
   B . . . .

5

Example
STUDENT A I probably won't be seeing **Sally** again.
STUDENT B Never mind. I'll say good-bye to **her** for **you.**

1 A They . . . . . . Mrs Dilworth . . . .
   B . . . .
2 A We . . . . . . the children . . . .
   B . . . .
3 A Joe . . . . . . Brenda . . . .
   B . . . .
4 A Mary . . . . . . Dick . . . .
   B . . . .

¹ drop us a line: write to us

35 Television

Three TV programmes can be received in most parts of the U.K. – in colour by those with colour TV sets. The two BBC programmes (BBC 1 and BBC 2) do not carry advertisements, but the third channel (IBA) is commercially run.

	(i)	(ii)	(iii)	(iv)
A	Is there anything worth watching on the other channel?	Do you happen to know what's on after the news?	Do you remember what comes on next?	What's on BBC 2 at eight o'clock?
B	I think it's a western.	I've got a feeling it's a documentary.	I believe there's a variety show on.	As far as I can remember there's a quiz programme.
A	Do you mind if we switch over?	Does anybody mind if I watch it?	We mustn't miss that.	Would you mind if I watched it?
B	Well, I rather wanted to see the football match.	Don't you want to see part two of the serial?	Let me look in the 'Radio Times'[1] first.	No, I've been looking forward to it all evening.

[1] Radio Times: a weekly magazine giving details of BBC radio and TV programmes

I

Example

Don't switch the boxing off. I've been looking forward to watching it all day.

1) .... Panorama ....
2) ...... turn ....
3) .... seeing ....
4) .... the show ....
5) .... hearing ....

2

Example

STUDENT A Do you mind if we watch the **documentary** on **BBC 1**?

STUDENT B Actually, 'I rather wanted to see the **play** on **ITV**.

1 A ...... news ...... BBC 2?
  B ...... film ...... BBC 1.
2 A .... cartoons ...... ITV?
  B ...... cricket ...... BBC 2.
3 A ...... weather forecast .. BBC 1?
  B ...... quiz ...... ITV.
4 A ...... discussion ...... ITV?
  B ...... jazz concert ...... BBC 2.
5 A ...... serial ...... ITV?
  B ...... comedy ...... BBC 1.

3 ◉

Example

STUDENT A What's on **BBC 1** tonight at **8.30**?

STUDENT B As far as I can remember, it's **a play**.

1 A .... ITV .... 6.20?
  B .... a serial.
2 A .... Luxembourg .... eleven?
  B .... Top Twenty.
3 A .... the other side .... after the news?
  B .... a film.

4 A .... Southern ... before the quiz?
  B .... Coronation Street.
5 A .... Radio 3 .... after the Russian lessons?
  B .... a concert.

4 *

Reply to A's questions using the phrase 'I've got a feeling' and the correct auxiliary verb. (A should use a rising intonation to show doubt.)

Example

STUDENT A The weather forecast was on before the news, wasn't it?

STUDENT B **Was it?** I've got a feeling **it was on after the news.**

1 A The film's on at 8.30, isn't it?
  B .... at 9.30.
2 A The Radio Times comes out on Saturday, doesn't it?
  B .... on Friday.
3 A The football results are on Radio 1, aren't they?
  B .... Radio 4.
4 A The Queen spoke on Boxing Day, didn't she?
  B .... on Christmas Day.
5 A It's the 20th today, isn't it?
  B .... the 27th.

5 *◉

Reply to A's questions using the phrase 'nothing worth' plus a gerund.

Example

STUDENT A Why don't you **listen to the radio**?

STUDENT B There's nothing worth **listening to.**

1 A .... watch TV?
  B ....
2 A .... read a paper?
  B ....
3 A .... look at a magazine?
  B ....
4 A .... see a film?
  B ....
5 A .... buy something?
  B ....

36 *Thanks for Hospitality*

Flowers, given to the hostess on arrival, are always appreciated by English families offering hospitality. The wrapping paper should not be removed.

	(i)	(ii)	(iii)	(iv)
A	It's time we were off.	I really must be going now.	I think it's about time we made a move.[1]	If you'll excuse me, I really should be off now.
B	So soon? Can't you stay a little longer?	But you've only just come. Wouldn't you like to stay for a snack?[1]	What already? Won't you have another coffee?	Not yet surely. Have another drink at least.
A	I wish I could, but I'm late already.	That's very kind of you, but I mustn't be too late.	I'd love to, but I have to be up early tomorrow.	No, thank you all the same.
B	What a shame!	What a pity!	Oh dear! What a shame!	Oh dear! What a pity!
A	Thank you for a wonderful meal.	Thanks very much for the party.	Thank you for a most enjoyable evening.	Thank you very much indeed for the delicious meal.
B	I'm glad you enjoyed it.	It was a pleasure to have you.	Not at all. Hope you can come again.	Thank you for coming.

[1] a snack: a light meal

[1] made a move: started to go

I

Drills

Example

If you'll excuse me, I really ought to be on my way now.

1) . . . . leaving . . . .
2) . . . . have . . . .
3) . . . . must be . . . . . .
4) . . . . off . . . .
5) . . . . should be . . . . . .

2

Example

STUDENT A Do you have to go? Can't you **stay?**

STUDENT B I'd love to, but I really think it's about time I **left.**

1   A . . . . . . stay for tea?
     B . . . . was going.
2   A . . . . . stay a lttle longer?
     B . . . . was off.
3   A . . . . . stay for supper?
     B . . . . was on my way.
4   A . . . . . . stop?
     B . . . . made a move.
5   A . . . . . stay and have a meal?
     B . . . . went.

3 *◉

Respond to A's requests using a gerund.

Example

STUDENT A Tell John we're grateful that he **came.**

STUDENT B Thanks very much for **coming,** John.

1   A . . . . helped.
     B . . . .
2   A . . . . told us.
     B . . . .

3   A . . . . replied.
     B . . . .
4   A . . . . rang us.
     B . . . .
5   A . . . . reminded us.
     B . . . .

4 *◉

Respond to the statements by A with the correct form of the verb after 'I wish'.

Example

STUDENT A I won't stay for tea, thank you all the same.

STUDENT B What a pity! I wish you **would.**

1   A I can't stay for lunch, I'm afraid.
     B . . . .
2   A I don't get much free time, I'm sorry to say.
     B . . . .
3   A I haven't got time for a coffee, thank you all the same.
     B . . . .
4   A I'm not free again until next month, I'm afraid.
     B . . . .
5   A I won't have another coffee, thank you all the same.
     B . . . .

5 *◉

Respond to A's statements using the phrase 'It's time' plus the past tense.

Example

STUDENT A I haven't written to Mother for several weeks.

STUDENT B It's time you wrote to Mother.

1   A Alice hasn't washed her hair for at least a month.
     B . . . .
2   A They haven't done any gardening for over a fortnight.
     B . . . .
3   A I haven't taken my wife out for two or three months.
     B . . . .
4   A He hasn't had an early night for over a week.
     B . . . .
5   A They haven't been on holiday for more than a year.
     B . . . .

37 Asking People to Repeat and Offering Lifts in a Car

Do not say 'please' when you want somebody to repeat a sentence.

Hitch-hiking is generally considered to be easy in the U.K., and can be made even easier by displaying a foreign flag on a rucksack.

	(i)	(ii)	(iii)	(iv)
A	Sorry, but I didn't quite catch that.	I beg your pardon.	I'm afraid I didn't quite hear what you said.	Sorry, but I missed that.
B	I said, 'Can I give you a lift?'[1]	I said, 'Shan't I drive you home?'	I said, 'There's no rush, I can take you in the car.'	I said, 'I'll run you back in the car.'
A	Isn't it out of your way?	Won't it be putting you out?[1]	Won't it make you late?	Are you sure it's not too much trouble?
B	No, it's on my way home.	No, I can go that way round just as easily.	No, I'm going right past your place.	No, it won't take a minute to drop you off.

[1] give you a lift: take you in my car

[1] putting you out: inconveniencing you

1

Example

I'm sorry but I didn't quite catch what you were saying.

1) . . . . said.
2) Excuse me. . . . .
3) . . . . hear . . . .
4) I'm afraid . . . .
5) . . . . get . . . .

2

Example

STUDENT A Excuse me, but are you going anywhere near **Harrods?**

STUDENT B Yes, right **past it**. Can I **give you a lift?**

1 A . . . . Guildford?
  B . . . . through . . . . drop you off?
2 A . . . . the frontier?
  B . . . . up to . . . . drive you there?
3 A . . . . my place?
  B . . . . by . . . . run you back?
4 A . . . . the Severn Bridge?
  B . . . . over . . . . give you a lift?
5 A . . . . the railway arch?
  B . . . . under . . . . take you there?

3*◉

A changes his direct questions into indirect questions beginning with 'I asked if'.

Example

STUDENT A Do you want a lift?
STUDENT B I'm afraid I missed that.
STUDENT A I asked if you wanted a lift.

---

1 A Can I run you home?
  B Sorry, but I didn't catch that.
  A . . . .
2 A Is it on your way home?
  B I beg your pardon.
  A . . . .
3 A Isn't it too much trouble?
  B I'm afraid I didn't quite hear what you said.
  A . . . .
4 A Will it make you late?
  B Would you mind repeating that, please?
  A . . . .

4*

Reply to A's questions using the correct adverb.

Example

STUDENT A Isn't it **easier** for you to **go by train?**

STUDENT B No, I can **catch the bus** just as **easily.**

1 A . . . . better . . . . come on Monday?
  B . . . . leave it till Tuesday . . . .

Drills

2 A . . . . cheaper . . . . hitch-hike?
  B . . . . go by bike . . . .
3 A . . . . quicker . . . . fly direct?
  B . . . . go via Rome . . . .
4 A . . . . more convenient . . . . take the M1?[1]
  B . . . . follow the A1[2] . . . .
5 A . . . . simpler . . . . go alone?
  B . . . . take you with me . . . .

5*

Example

STUDENT A Are **we** going to **him?**

STUDENT B No, **he's** driving over to **our** place.

1 A . . . . . . he . . . . . . you?
  B . . . .
2 A . . . . . . they . . . . . . her?
  B . . . .
3 A . . . . John . . . . them?
  B . . . . •• . . . .
4 A . . . . . . she . . . . . . Fred?
  B . . . .

[1] M1: motorways in the U.K. are given the letter M
[2] A1: main roads in the U.K. are given the letter A

38 *Asking Favours*

English people use rather elaborate, roundabout ways of asking for things, and some foreigners therefore may appear rude because they are more direct than the English tend to be. The most important thing about asking favours of people is *how* you ask, what intonation you use, rather than the actual words you use. When it seems likely that the other person will refuse, the question can be phrased so that the refusal does not cause embarrassment.

	(i)	(ii)	(iii)	(iv)
A	Is there any chance of borrowing your typewriter?	Would you mind if I had some time off?	Do you think I could possibly have my meals a little earlier?	I wonder whether you could put my friend up[1] for a few days?
B	How long for?	When exactly?	That would depend on when.	Tell me when.
A	Until the end of the week.	Monday and Tuesday of next week.	Just over Easter.	Next weekend actually.
B	Yes, I think that would be all right.	I'd like to say yes, but it's just not possible.	I'll have to check with my wife first.	Let me think it over, and I'll tell you later.

[1] put my friend up: give my friend a bed

I

Example

    I wonder whether I could possibly borrow your new car.

1) .... have next Saturday off.
2) Do you think .... ?
3) .... invite Sally to your party?
4) .... round to tea?
5) I wonder whether ....

2*

Reply to A's questions using the phrase 'No, go right ahead'.

Example

STUDENT A Would you mind if I **closed** the window?

STUDENT B No, go right ahead and **close** it.

1 A ...... turned the TV on?
  B ....
2 A ...... turned the radio down?
  B ....
3 A ...... made myself a cup of tea?
  B ....
4 A ...... had a bath?
  B ....
5 A ...... used your tools?
  B ....

3

Instead of saying: 'Don't smoke' it is more polite to say 'I'd rather you didn't smoke, if you don't mind'. Change A's orders to a more polite form.

Example

STUDENT A Don't **smoke**.

STUDENT B I'd rather you didn't **smoke**, if you don't mind.

1 A ...... play the piano.
  B ....
2 A ...... do your washing in the kitchen.
  B ....
3 A ...... shut the window.
  B ....
4 A ...... use my sewing machine.
  B ....
5 A ...... smoke in bed.
  B ....

4⊚

Instead of saying: 'Can I borrow your bicycle?' it is more polite to say: 'I wonder whether I could borrow your bicycle'. Change A's questions to a more polite form.

Example

STUDENT A Can I **borrow your tent**?

STUDENT B I wonder whether I could **borrow your tent**.

1 A ...... have an early breakfast?
  B ....
2 A ...... invite some friends round?
  B ....
3 A ...... make a telephone call?
  B ....
4 A ...... change my day off?
  B ....
5 A ...... have a bath?
  B ....

5⊚

Instead of saying: 'Can you do some shopping for me?' it is more polite to say: 'Do you think you could possibly do some shopping for me?'

Change A's questions to a more polite form.

Example

STUDENT A Can you **do some shopping for me**?

STUDENT B Do you think you could possibly **do some shopping for me**?

1 A ...... teach me to drive?
  B .... ?
2 A ...... put me up for the night?
  B .... ?
3 A ... help me with this letter?
  B .... ?
4 A ...... lend me a pound?
  B. .... ?
5 A ...... show me the way?
  B .... ?

39 Complaining

The English are reluctant to complain, and when they do so it is often in a somewhat apologetic manner. All the examples given here are rather strong.

	(i)	**(ii)**	**(iii)**	**(iv)**
A	I wish you wouldn't have your TV so loud.	Do you think you could keep the noise down a bit?	That radio's terribly loud. Could you turn it down a fraction?	Do you have to have that record on quite so loud?[1]
B	Sorry! Were you trying to sleep?	Sorry! Have I been keeping you awake?	Sorry! Is it disturbing you?	Sorry! Is it bothering you?
A	Yes, and while I think of it – please ask when you borrow the iron.	Yes, and another thing – would you mind not using my toothpaste?	Yes, and something else – wouldn't it be an idea to buy your own soap?[1]	Yes, and while I'm about it – please don't use the phone without asking.
B	I really ought to have known better. Sorry!	I'm sorry. I thought you didn't mind.	Sorry! I didn't realise you felt so strongly about it.	So sorry! I meant to ask you, but you were out.

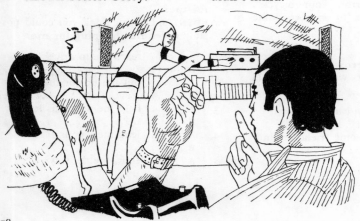

[1] Wouldn't it be a good idea to buy your own soap?: rather sarcastic

[1] Do you have to have that record on quite so loud?: rather sarcastic

1

Example

I 'do wish you wouldn't forget to switch the hall light out.

1) .... wipe your feet on the mat.
2) .... would remember ....
3) Do you think you could ....?
4) .... leave the bathroom tidy?
5) Wouldn't it be a good idea ....?

2

Example

STUDENT A Do you think you could **make a little less noise?**

STUDENT B Sorry, I didn't realise you **were trying to sleep.**

1 A ...... take your shoes off?
  B ...... had just done the floor.
2 A ...... turn the radio down?
  B ...... were in bed already.
3 A ...... hurry up in the bathroom?
  B ...... were waiting to come in.
4 A ...... drive a little slower?
  B ...... were a nervous passenger.
5 A ...... shave in the bathroom?
  B ...... wanted me to do it there.

3◉

Change A's statements so that they begin with 'I do wish you wouldn't ... '

Example

STUDENT A Don't **leave the doors open.**

STUDENT B I do wish you wouldn't **leave the doors open.**

1 A Don't run off all the hot water.
  B ....
  A Don't read the newspaper at breakfast.
  B ....

3 A Don't slam the front door.
  B ....
4 A Don't leave the bath so dirty.
  B ....
5 A Don't forget to turn off the hall light.
  B ....

4*◉

Change A's statements using the phrase 'Would you mind' plus a gerund.

Example

STUDENT A Tell Sue **to wipe** her feet before she comes in.

STUDENT B Would you mind **wiping** your feet before you come in, Sue?

1 A Tell Sue not to use her saucer as an ash-tray.
  B ....?
2 A Tell Sue not to let the bath overflow.
  B ....?
3 A Tell Sue to ask before she uses the phone.
  B ....?
4 A Tell Sue not to smoke in bed.
  B ....?
5 A Tell Sue to phone when she's going to be late for lunch.
  B ....?

5*

You can say: 'You can't use the typewriter unless you ask' or: 'You can't use the typewriter without asking'.

Change A's statements using the word 'without' plus a gerund.

Example

STUDENT A You can't use the typewriter **unless you ask.**

STUDENT B You can't use the typewriter **without asking.**

1 A You can't drive a car unless you have a licence.
  B ....
2 A You can't have an early breakfast unless you tell me first.
  B ....
3 A You can't iron unless you put a blanket on the table.
  B ....
4 A You can't pay by cheque unless you leave your name and address.
  B ....
5 A You can't go unless you say goodbye.
  B ....

40 Apologising

The phrase 'seem to have' is often heard in apologies when things have been mislaid (temporarily lost). This is because it gives the idea of doubt, and the speaker wishes to break the news gently to the owner and not to alarm him too much. Sometimes it is also used when things have been lost, or even broken!

	(i)	(ii)	(iii)	(iv)
A	I'm afraid I've spilt ink all over the table-cloth.	I'm 'awfully sorry, but I seem to have mislaid your scarf.	I'm very much afraid I've burned a hole in the rug.	I'm 'dreadfully sorry, but I've broken a plate.
B	Oh, never mind about that.	Oh, don't worry about that.	Oh, that's all right.	Oh, that doesn't matter.
A	I'm 'terribly sorry. Won't you let me pay for it?	I just don't know what to say. I'll replace it, of course.	I 'do apologise. I'll buy you a new one first thing on Monday.	I'm 'ever so[1] sorry. Tell me where you bought it so I can get you another.
B	No, I won't hear of it.	No, that's quite out of the question.	Of course not. I never 'did like it anyway.	No, certainly not. I wouldn't dream of letting you do that.

[1] ever so: very

orry, but I'm afraid I've burned a hole in the carpet.

. . . . broken your alarm clock.

. . . . lost my front door key.

. . . . let the bath overflow.

. . . . mislaid your umbrella.

. . . . run over your cat.

. . . rribly sorry, but I seem

. . your old school tie.

. . . quite all right. I never

. . anyway.

. . n your Skegness sou-

. . ay.

. . ash-tray . . . . . .

. . our Robin Hood hat.

. . hat . . . . . .

. . ound your cuckoo clock.

. . that . clock . . . . . .

. . ged your plastic flowers.

. . se flowers . . . . . .

5   A   . . . . driven over that china gnome[1] outside.

   B   . . . . . . that gnome . . . . . .

3

Reply to A's questions using the phrase 'ever so' and the appropriate adjective.

Example

STUDENT A Will it be **easy** to get a new one?

STUDENT B Yes, it'll be ever so **easy.**

1   A   Are they annoyed with you?

   B   . . . .

2   A   Is he upset by it?

   B   . . . .

3   A   Was he apologetic?

   B   . . . .

4   A   Were you sorry for her?

   B   . . . .

5   A   Are you pleased with it?

   B   . . . .

4*

Reply to A's questions using the phrase 'I wouldn't dream of' plus a gerund.

Example

STUDENT A Will you **apologise to him?**

STUDENT B No, I wouldn't dream of **apologising to him.**

1   A   . . . . . . keep it a secret?

   B   . . . .

2   A   . . . . . . let him pay for it?

   B   . . . .

3   A   . . . . . . try to repair it?

   B   . . . .

4   A   . . . . . . let her replace it?

   B   . . . .

5   A   . . . . . . complain?

   B   . . . .

5⦾

Respond to A's questions using the emphatic form.

Example

STUDENT A Why didn't you apologise?

STUDENT B **But I did apologise.**

1   A   Why don't you believe it?

   B   . . . .

2   A   Why doesn't he understand?

   B   . . . .

3   A   Why don't you feel sorry?

   B   . . . .

4   A   Why didn't you replace it?

   B   . . . .

5   A   Why doesn't she know about it?

   B   . . . .

[1] some English people decorate their gardens with small statues

41 What Shall We Do This Evening (1)

For the foreign visitor interested in sport, local clubs are excellent places in which to meet English people. There is normally a club for each sport in every town; the secretary's name and address can be obtained from the town information office.

	(i)	(ii)	(iii)	(iv)
A	How would you like to come bowling?	Do you fancy a game of tennis?	Feel like a stroll in the park?	Let's go ice-skating.
B	I'm not overkeen,[1] actually.	It's nice of you to ask, but I don't think so.	I don't think I will, thanks all the same.	No, I'm really not in the mood for it this evening.
A	What about a Chinese meal, then?	Well, how about coming to see Tony?	Come on. A spot of exercise would do us good.	Then why don't we just go out for a coffee?
B	No, I thought I'd have an evening at home for a change.	No, I honestly can't afford the time.	No, if you don't mind I think I'll stay in tonight.	No, really. I've promised myself an early night.

[1] I'm not overkeen: I don't want to (a typical understatement)

82

I

Drills

Example
    They're not dreadfully keen on going out: they want an evening by the fire.

1) She   ... very   ....   she   ... a morning at home.
2) We   ... awfully   ....   we   ... a day in the garden.
3) I   ... terribly   I   ... an early night.
4) He   ... over   ....   he   ... a lie-in.[1]

2◉

Example
STUDENT A Won't you join us for a game of **cards**?
STUDENT B No, thanks. I'm really not in the mood for **cards** this evening.

1 A .... tennis?
   B ....
2 A .... darts?
   B ....
3 A .... billiards?
   B ....
4 A .... table tennis?
   B ....
5 A .... bridge?
   B ....

3

Example
STUDENT A Do you fancy a game of **tennis**?
STUDENT B No, let's go **swimming** for a change.

1 A ...... chess?
   B ...... dancing ......
2 A ...... cards?
   B ...... skating ......
3 A ...... football?
   B ...... riding ......
4 A ...... draughts?
   B ...... bowling ......

4*◉

Reply to A's questions using the phrase 'How about ....' plus a gerund.

Example
STUDENT A Ask **Tony** if **he** wants to **play tennis**.
STUDENT B How about **playing tennis Tony**?

1 A .... Joe .... stay at home.
   B ....?
2 A .... Sue .... come for a stroll.
   B ....?
3 A .. the boys ... watch the football.
   B ....?
4 A .. the girls ... go out for a meal.
   B ....?
5 A .... Margaret .... walk along the sea-front.
   B ....?

5*◉

You can say 'Exercise is healthy' or 'Exercise does you good'.
Reply to A's questions using the phrase 'do/does you good' in the affirmative or negative.

Examples
STUDENT A Is exercise healthy?
STUDENT B Yes, it does you good.
STUDENT A Are cigarettes healthy?
STUDENT B No, they don't do you any good.

1 A Are apples healthy?
   B ....
2 A Is fresh air healthy?
   B ....
3 A Are late nights healthy?
   B ....
4 A Is strong coffee healthy?
   B ....
5 A Is orange juice healthy?
   B ....

[1] a lie-in: from the verb 'to lie in bed'

42 What Shall We Do This Evening (2)

English people, especially the younger ones, frequently take bottles of drink with them to parties and give them to the host on arrival. They are then put with the other bottles for everybody to drink. A bottle of spirits or wine, or several bottles of beer are suitable. It is sometimes difficult to know what is a real invitation and what is not! "You really must come and see us one of these days" is probably not a genuine invitation. The best tactic is to reply "Thank you very much. I love meeting English people" and then wait to see whether a specific date is mentioned.

	(i)	(ii)	(iii)	(iv)
A	How about coming out for a drink with me this evening?	Why don't we go for a drive in the country?	Do you feel like going to the cinema?	Would you like to come to a party with me tonight?
B	I'd like that very much. Thank you.	That would be very nice. Thank you.	That sounds like a good idea. Thank you.	I'd love to. Thank you very much.
A	Shall we say round about eight?	I'll pick you up about 7.30.	Let's make it 6.30 at your place.	I'll call round for you after supper.
B	Fine. See you then.	Right. See you later.	That'll be OK by me.	OK. I'll be ready.

1

Example
Would you like to come to a football match with me tonight?

1) . . . . barbecue[1]
2) . . . . ?
3) Do you feel like coming . . . .
4) . . . . dance
5) . . . . . . fancy . . . .

    . . . . ?
    . . . . . . on Saturday?
    . . . . ?
    . . . . ?
    . . . . ?

2

Example
STUDENT A How about **going to see 'Dr Zhivago'?**
STUDENT B That sounds like a good idea. It's a long time since we **saw a good film.**

1 A . . . . . . going to the 'Grand' for dinner?
  B . . . . had a good meal.
2 A . . . . . . inviting John and Maggie round?
  B . . . . had any visitors.
3 A . . . . . . walking down to the Rose and Crown[2]?
  B . . . . went out for a drink.
4 A . . . . . . taking a bus to Speakers' Corner[3]?
  B . . . . had a good argument.
5 A . . . . . . asking Brian and Sam over for bridge?
  B . . . . played a hand of cards.

3 ◉

(B should use a rising intonation.)

Example
STUDENT A What's the best time to **meet?**
STUDENT B Shall we say round about **eight?**

1 A . . . . call round?
  B . . . . 7.30?
2 A . . . . start back?
  B . . . . midnight?
3 A . . . . pick you up?
  B . . . . 4 o'clock?
4 A . . . . leave?
  B . . . . ten to four?
5 A . . . . call for you?
  B . . . . seven?

4 ◉

Example
STUDENT A Can **you and your wife** be ready at **8.30?**
STUDENT B Yes, **8.30** will be OK by **us.**

1 A . . . . . . Mary . . . . . . six?
  B . . . .
2 A . . . . . . they . . . . . seven-fifteen?
  B . . . .

3

3 A . . . . . . you . . . . 7.30?
  B
4 A . . . . Timothy . . . . . . 1.15?
  B . . . .
5 A . . . . . the girls . . . . . . eleven?
  B . . . .

5 *◉

Example
STUDENT A Do you feel like **eating out?**
STUDENT B That's a good idea. We haven't **eaten out** for ages.

1 A . . . . seeing a film?
  B
2 A . . . . playing tennis?
  B
3 A . . . . driving up to London?
  B
4 A . . . . going skating?
  B
5 A . . . . having a party?
  B

[1] barbecue: a picnic where food is cooked over an open fire
[2] Rose and Crown: a typical pub name (see 13)
[3] Speakers' Corner: at Hyde Park in London

43 Complimenting People on Clothes

It is normally only the younger Englishmen that compliment each other on clothes.

	(i)	(ii)	(iii)	(iv)
A	What a nice skirt!	I 'say, I like your new rain-coat.	You're looking very smart in that new coat.	That's a very nice blazer you're wearing.
B	Does it look all right?	Is it a good fit?	Does it suit me?	Do you really like it?
A	Yes, and it matches your scarf perfectly.	Yes, it looks fabulous.	Yes, and I like the colour, too.	Yes, and it goes well with your new pullover, too.
B	I got it for £9.30 in a sale.[1]	It only cost me £7.80.	You know I only paid £10 for it.	You'll never believe it, but it only cost £8.50.
A	It's incredible.	Well, that was very good value.	You got a bargain there.	Very reasonable indeed.

[1] a sale: when goods are sold cheaply in the shops – often in spring and autumn

1

Example

I 'say, those're very nice-looking gloves you've got on.

1) .... smart   ....
2) .... shoes ....
3) .... you're wearing.
4) ......that's a .... jacket ....
5) .... elegant ....

2

Example

Your umbrella matches your raincoat marvellously.

1   ... jumper ... trousers beautifully.
2   ... gloves ... handbag perfectly.
3   ... slacks ... cardigan fabulously.
4   ... belt ... scarf superbly.
5   ... socks ... sandals exactly.

3

Example

STUDENT A What do you think of my new **raincoat**?

STUDENT B It looks **fabulous**.

1   A .... suit?
     B .... very smart.
2   A .... tie?
     B .... great.
3   A .... shoes?
     B .... very nice.
4   A .... jacket?
     B .... marvellous.
5   A .... skirt?
     B .... gorgeous.

4*

Example

STUDENT A Do you think this **blouse** really suits me?

STUDENT B Of course **it does. It goes** well with your **scarf**, too.

1   A ...... pullover ......?
     B ...... trousers ......
2   A ...... false eye-lashes ......?
     B ...... hair-style ......
3   A ...... shirt ......?
     B ...... tie ......
4   A ...... stockings ......?
     B ..... shoes ......
5   A ...... hat ......?
     B ...... handbag ......

5⊚

Reply to A's questions using the word 'jolly'.

Example

STUDENT A Don't you think that's a **good** match?

STUDENT B Yes, it's 'jolly **good**.

1   A .... a reasonable price?
     B ....
2   A .... a nice colour?
     B ....
3   A .... a smart coat?
     B ....
4   A .... a good fit?
     B ....
5   A .... a clever design?
     B ....

44 *The Weather*

Foreigners are often amused that the English spend so much time discussing the weather. The reason for this is not simply that our weather is interesting and variable, but that the English are reluctant to converse about personal matters with people who are not friends. Mentioning the weather can be a useful and inoffensive way of starting a conversation with a stranger at a bus-stop or in a train.

	(i)	(ii)	(iii)	(iv)
A	Fairly mild for the time of year.	It seems to be clearing up.	Nice and bright this morning.	It's good to see the sun again.
B	Yes. Quite different from the forecast.	It makes a change, doesn't it?	Yes. Much better than yesterday.	A big improvement on what we've been having.
A	They[1] say we're in for snow.[2]	Apparently it's going to turn colder.	The wind'll probably get up later.	It's supposed to cloud over this afternoon.
B	Let's hope it keeps fine for the weekend.	Still, another month should see us through the worst of it.[1]	As long as it doesn't rain.[1]	I didn't think it would last.

[1] They: the forecasters
[2] we're in for snow: snow is expected

[1] see us through the worst of it: find us through the worst of the winter and into spring

[1] as long as it doesn't rain: I don't mind what happens provided it doesn't rain

I

Example

Apparently it's going to turn colder and freeze later on.

1) . . . . drizzle . . . . . .

2) They say . . . .

3) . . . . warmer . . . .

4) . . . . get . . . .

5) . . . . rain . . . . . .

2

Example

STUDENT A They say we're in for **snow**.

STUDENT B As long as it doesn't **rain**.

1 A . . . . . . fog.

   B . . . . . freeze.

2 A . . . . . . drizzle.

   B . . . . . snow.

3 A . . . . . . high winds.

   B . . . . . last.

4 A . . . . . . thunder.

   B . . . . . spoil the weekend.

5 A . . . . . . showers.

   B . . . . . interrupt the cricket.

3⊚

Respond to the statements by 'A' using the comparative form of the adjective.

Example

STUDENT A **Cold** this morning, isn't it?

STUDENT B Yes. Apparently it's going to get even **colder**.

1 A Hot . . . .?

   B . . . .

2 A Warm . . . .?

   B . . . .

3 A Cool . . . .?

   B . . . .

4 A Wet . . . .?

   B . . . .

5 A Foggy . . . .?

   B . . . .

4*⊚

Example

STUDENT A I think **the wind's getting stronger**.

STUDENT B Yes, they said **it would get stronger** later on.

1 A . . . . the weather's turned colder.

   B . . . .

2 A . . . . it's coming over cloudy.

   B . . . .

3 A . . . . the fog's got thicker.

   B . . . .

4 A . . . . it's turned milder.

   B . . . .

5 A . . . . it's got warmer.

   B . . . .

Key to Drills

1
[*Drill 3*]
Can you tell me how far it is to London, please? / where the shops·are / which direction the motorway is / how many mlies it is to the nearest garage / which way the coast is
[*Drill 4*]
It'll take her ten lessons to learn it. / them half an hour to walk it / me twenty minutes to make it / us twenty-four hours to deliver it / you less than a minute to get there
[*Drill 5*]
It's too foggy to see the turning. / too wet to go on foot / too dark to find the way / too late to get there in time / too difficult to remember

2
[*Drill 3*]
You 'shouldn't have got out at the park. / caught a Red Arrow / come early / asked for the station / bought a return ticket
[*Drill 4*]
You 'should have remembered the number. / brought your season ticket / rung the bell / had some change / got a return

8
[*Drill 4*]
Because I was in a hurry. / they were / she is / they are / he was / we are / we were

9
[*Drill 3*]
I've had 'far too many already. / much / many / much / much
[*Drill 5*]
No, they hardly wanted anything. / drank / ate / cost / got

10
[*Drill 4*]
I'd love it. / some / them / to / one

11
[*Drill 5*]
Two teas and a coffee, please. / a Coca Cola and four teas / three chocolates and two orange juices / an orange juice and two milks / three black coffees

12
[*Drill 4*]
I've already had it, thank you very much. / seen it / booked it / tasted it / chosen it

13
[*Drill 4*]
I don't 'think they do. / it was / she does / they have / there is

14
[*Drill 3*]
No, you smoked one of hers. / he . . . . theirs / they . . . . ours / she . . . . yours / he . . . . hers
[*Drill 4*]
Yes, I've cut down. / I'll cut down / I gave up / I'm going to give up / I had to give up / I had to cut down

15
[*Drill 5*]
I want a twin-bedded room. / the blue-eyed waitress / a two-roomed suite / the red-carpeted room / the long-haired waiter

18
[*Drill 5*]
Yes, I've done quite a bit of gardening. / waiting / translating / office cleaning / fruit picking

20
[*Drill 3*]
Yes, I'd like my nails manicured. / moustache trimmed / beard shaved off / parting moved / the top thinned out

21
[*Drill 5*]
Yes, I'm being looked after, thank you. / being attended to / being seen to / being taken care of

22
[*Drill 3*]
You can sit wherever you like. / wear whatever / come however / bring whoever / come whenever
[*Drill 4*]
would you? / do you / have you / were there / is there /
[*Drill 5*]
can't I? / doesn't he / didn't you / is there / didn't they

23
[*Drill 3*]
'I've only been given three. / 'I'll only be given / 'I'd only been given / 'I'd only be given

/ 'I'm only going to be given / 'I'm only given / 'I'm only being given

25
[*Drill 4*]
Who are they thinking of? / What are they apologising about / Where are they calling from / Who are they talking to / What are they looking for

26
[*Drill 4*]
I think they've already left. / he's already phoned / she's already had lunch / they've already come back / he's already rung

27
[*Drill 3*]
Did you go anywhere else? / buy anything else / write to anyone else / post anything else / phone any one else

28
[*Drill 4*]
Yes, she 'must have eaten it. / they 'must have taken it / I 'must have done it / he 'must have understood / she 'must have broken it

29
[*Drill 5*]
By the feel of it, it's broken. / By the smell of it / By the sound of it / By the taste of it / By the look of it

30
[*Drill 4*]
'I'm being given cream. / 'I'll be given / 'I've been given / 'I'm given / 'I was being given / 'I'd be given / 'I'd been given

31
[*Drill 5*]
I haven't seen it since breakfast. / for / since / for / for

33
[*Drill 4*]
She's gone to her sister's / She's at / They'll go to / He was at / You've got to go to
[*Drill 5*]
Wasn't 'I invited, too? / Won't \ Shan't /
'I be invited / Aren't 'I being invited / Wasn't 'I being invited / Oughtn't 'I to be invited

35
[*Drill 4*]
Is it? I've got a feeling it's on at 9.30. / Does it / Are they / Did she / Is it
[*Drill 5*]
There's nothing worth watching. / worth reading / worth looking at / worth seeing / worth buying

36
[*Drill 3*]
Thanks very much for helping, John. / telling us / replying / ringing us / reminding us
[*Drill 4*]
What a pity! I wish you could. / you did / you had / you were / you would
[*Drill 5*]
It's time she washed her hair. / they did some gardening / you took your wife out / he had an early night / they went on holiday

37
[*Drill 3*]
I asked if I could run you home. / if it was on your way home / if it wasn't too much trouble / if it would make you late

[*Drill 4*]
No, I can leave it till Tuesday just as well. / just as cheaply / just as quickly / just as conveniently / just as simply
[*Drill 5*]
No, I'm driving over to his place. / she .... their / they .... his / he .... her

38
[*Drill 2*]
No, go right ahead and turn it on. / turn it down / make yourself one / have one / use them

39
[*Drill 4*]
Would you mind not using your saucer as an ash-tray, Sue. / not letting / asking / not smoking / phoning
[*Drill 5*]
You can't drive a car without having a licence. / without telling / without putting / without leaving / without saying

40
[*Drill 4*]
No, I wouldn't dream of keeping it a secret. / letting / trying / letting / complaining

41
[Drill 4]
How about staying at home,
Joe? / coming for / watching /
going out / walking along
[Drill 5]
Yes, they do you good. / it does
you good / No, they don't do
you any good / it doesn't do you
any good / it does you good

42
[Drill 5]
That's a good idea. We haven't
seen a film for ages. / played
tennis / driven up to London /
been skating / had a party

43
[Drill 4]
Of course it does. It goes well
with your new trousers, too. /
they do. They go well with /
it does. It goes well / they do.
They go well with / it does. It
goes well with

44
[Drill 4]
Yes, they said it would turn
colder later on. / come over
cloudy / get thicker / turn
milder / get warmer

LONGMAN GROUP
LIMITED, LONDON
Associated companies,
branches and representatives
throughout the world
© LONGMAN GROUP LTD 1972

*First published *1972*
*New impressions *1973 (thrice); *1974*
**1975 : *1976*

ISBN 0 582 52172 6

*Printed in Hong Kong by
Dai Nippon Printing Co (H.K.) Ltd*